The Faithful Steward:

Reclaiming Stewardship for Christ's Kingdom

Michael O'Hurley-Pitts, Ph.D.

Foreword by Tony Campolo, Ph.D.

Edited by Dick L. Kranendonk, Ed.D.

Originally published as *The Passionate Steward: Recovering Stewardship from Secular Fundraising*, St. Brigid Press, Toronto–2002. ISBN: 0-9731378-0-0

National Library of Canada Cataloguing in Publication

NAME(S): O'Hurley-Pitts, Michael, 1965–
          Canadian Council of Christian Charities

TITLE(S): The Faithful Steward: Reclaiming Stewardship for Christ's Kingdom / Michael O'Hurley-Pitts / Edited by Dick L. Kranendonk / Foreword by Tony Campolo.

PUBLISHER: Toronto: St. Brigid Press
NOTES: Co-published by Canadian Council of Christian Charities
           Includes bibliographical references and index.

NUMBERS: Canadiana: 20029060486

ISBN: 0-9731378-1-9

CLASSIFICATION: LC Call no.: BV772 O47 2003 Dewey:248/.6 21

SUBJECTS: Stewardship, Christian

Statistics Canada information is used with the permission of the Minister of Industry, as Minister responsible for Statistics Canada. Information on the availability of the wide range of data from Statistics Canada can be obtained from Statistics Canada's Regional Offices, its World Wide Web site at http://www.statcan.ca

All biblical quotations are from the New Revised Standard Version (NRSV) unless otherwise indicated.

About the Author

Michael O'Hurley-Pitts has been recognized for his unique talents and skills. He has helped shape the success of myriad projects for a wide spectrum of Churches, social institutions and other non-profit organizations. A respected leader in stewardship development, Michael has been an invited presenter at ecclesial and non-profit conferences and workshops for many organizations in the United States and Canada. He has also served as an expert commentator and analyst for national news broadcasts in Canada and the United States, where his opinions are highly regarded.

In 1999, Michael founded a stewardship consulting and leadership training firm—Faith Matters, Inc. In the past, he has served as a Senior Consultant for an international fundraising firm, and as a Development Officer in the Archdiocese of New York. He has also served in positions of trust and confidence in the United States Congress, and has won high praise for his leadership as an Executive Director of a national non-profit organization.

Michael has been regularly published in the professional journals *The Canadian Fundraiser* and *Gift Planning in Canada*. In addition, he publishes the online journal, *The Stewardship Review,* a quarterly journal of Christian stewardship and philanthropy.

Peer and Professional Book Reviews

"Michael O'Hurley Pitts offers an invitation for the reader to enter into a healthy critique of commonly accepted assumptions and practices in stewardship ministry. In contrasting secular fund-raising and Christian stewardship, this work provides a meaningful bridge between theological reflection and the faithful practice. It is a valuable contribution to the ongoing ecumenical dialogue on stewardship."

The Reverend Dr. Ed Taylor, Executive Director
Ecumenical Stewardship Center, Indianapolis, IN

"Over the years while I was involved in raising millions of dollars for the Anglican Church of Canada I had a nagging feeling that all was not well with the process. That is why I welcome... [the book] by Michael O'Hurley-Pitts... Far too often the question of money has been separated from the other two elements of stewardship: time and talent. It really becomes messy when they are substituted for each other. When this happens, our understanding of stewardship as an expression of our Christian profession is sadly compromised."

The Reverend Canon Gordon Baker
The Anglican Journal

"Typically books that focus on Christian financial stewardship start with a window dressing of Biblical thought and then move quickly to the real essence—methods of getting more money from the people for their cause. Though this book is written against the backdrop of declining funds flowing into the treasuries of mainline churches, true to the title, the author focuses on the steward as a person, not merely on the churches' need for more money.... The sub-title to the book... encapsulates the core thesis of the book. Drawing on his vast experience as a stewardship consultant both in the U.S. and Canada, his passion for the church, and his solid knowledge of Scripture, he urges the church to return to its Biblical roots. Instead of blaming secular fundraisers for getting it wrong, he challenges the church to assume the ongoing responsibility of doing it right."

The Messenger
(Evangelical Mennonite Conference Newspaper)

"[The book] reads more along the lines of a "why-not" or "how-about" book in that problems of parish stewardship are not addressed with definite solutions in mind, but are exposed to allow the reader to come to the proper conclusions about what is best for his/her church. O'Hurley-Pitts defines the various kinds of stewardship, pointing out foremost that giving is "not transactional," but "vocational"... People should want to give without having to be bombarded by a "what's in it for me" mentality, particularly when the incentives are hardly spiritual. For the struggling small-town parish or the established metropolis church, O'Hurley-Pitts lays out the nuts and bolts of stewardship in a concise and timely manner."

Catholic and Christian Book Reviews

"Michael O'Hurley-Pitts... in an articulate and passionate manner, calls the church to be true to its own message. He argues convincingly that Christian stewardship has little to do with funding budgets, naming opportunities, duty, or who gives the most. It is rather about the use of our time, talent and treasure individually and corporately, to engage in prayer, worship, mercy, kindness and acts of charity. Stewardship has to do with our generous response in praise and honour of our generous Creator God."

Religion Book Reviews

"This is an important work, relevant for those who live and work in the church community. [The book] illustrates that stewardship is much more than a donor's economic exchange or the management of their wealth. Stewardship has the qualities of faith and prayer."

Tom Cullinan, Esquire
Director, National Planned Giving Institute
College of William & Mary, Williamsburg, VA

"I particularly liked Michael's consistent emphasis on stewardship as a dynamic expression of our Christian life. [The book's] presentation of stewardship in terms of the journey of faith and of the faithful, and as an outward activity of inward grace and faith is compelling. Readers can reaffirm and reclaim a clear understanding of stewardship as that anchor out of which we live our lives as people of faith."

Priscilla S. Bizer, Vice President for Development
Andover Newton Theological School

"This is a spiritually sensitive and thoughtful book inviting Christians to re-evaluate how we give and promote giving. Recommended particularly to Church leaders."

CBA Marketplace Book Reviews
Christian Booksellers Association Magazine

"[The book] by Michael O'Hurley-Pitts gives a refreshing look at stewardship as true ministry. Not just another fund-raising manual for the church; rather, stewardship is understood as a personal commitment to Christ, actually living the Gospel and Liturgical life. Stewardship must be understood as a complete identity for the Christian. The whole Church of Jesus Christ is called to be a steward of God's mission on earth. As the Church engages in God's mission, we become identified, both Christian and Church, as true stewards. Our participation in mission grows out of true stewardship. God calls us to the work of missions because we are stewards. Once this understanding takes hold, funding our missions will no longer be a concern nor a problem, and there will be no further need for secularized gimmicks, something totally antithetical to the teachings of Christ. Michael O'Hurley-Pitts has captured the essence of this in his masterpiece."

Chris Andreas, Stewardship Administrator
Greek Orthodox Church, New York, New York

"[The book] raises some basic questions which it would be prudent for the Church to address as it faces the necessity for money to enable it to carry out its Mission in the world... I would strongly urge any person or group concerned about the growth, renewal, and transformation of the Church to read and discuss with others The Passionate Steward. The insights gained by doing so would make it clear that this was a wise use of the time involved."

The Most Reverend Edward W. Scott
Retired Primate
The Anglican Church of Canada

Contents

Index of Charts and Tables

Foreword

The church suffers because it has watered down the radical commitment that Jesus requires of his followers when it comes to giving, and has adapted to culturally prescribed levels of reasonableness. Dietrich Bonhoffer once said, "When Jesus calls a man, he bids him come and die." Unfortunately, most churches are not about to make the kind of calling that Jesus made readily obvious to its members for fear that they will be alienated by such a demand. At best, the churches call people to tithe.

Anyone who studies the scriptures knows that tithing is an Old Testament concept. The Jesus of the New Testament does not ask for one-tenth of what we have, but, instead, asks for total surrender and the yielding of all that one has for the work of Christ and His kingdom. But even when Christians do consider tithing to the work of the church, they often wonder whether they are making a wise investment. Churches often spend the financial resources that are placed in their hands in ways that are questionable. For instance, if Jesus had the choice between putting $100,000 into a new stained glass window or providing food and medicine for children suffering from AIDS in Africa, it is questionable that He would choose the stained glass window. So many of the expenditures of religious institutions foster reluctance on the part of givers as people ask, "Why should we sacrifice to support churches that are not themselves willing to sacrifice to meet the needs of the poor and the oppressed of the world?"

In order to sustain themselves, religious institutions have resorted to a host of fundraising techniques which they have learned from the secular business community. This book is about critiquing those techniques and calling churches back into a style of stewardship that is befitting biblical teachings and can inspire sacrifice among its members.

One time I had flown into Philadelphia on a "red-eye" from the West Coast. That is one of those flights where in you take off from California late in the evening and arrive in the East early in the morning. When I got off the plane at 8:30 a.m. I was met by my secretary, who then broke the news to me that I had a speaking engagement scheduled for ten that morning. She said, "I don't know how we missed this one. Somewhere along the line the notices of this engagement fell between the cracks. I wanted to be here to meet you because you need to be taken directly to the church. It's one of those World Day of Prayer services, and you're supposed to deliver a 'missionary' message."

We quickly drove to the church and when I took my place behind the pulpit I wasn't thinking clearly. I was too tired to be any place other than in bed. Consequently, I did not react as I should have when the woman leading the meeting announced to the several hundred women and handful of men who had gathered that she had a prayer request from a missionary in Venezuela. She described a wonderful doctor who had given her life to serving the poor in the barrios of Caracas. This missionary was pleading for five thousand dollars to put an addition onto her medical dispensary. The addition, she explained, was desperately needed because her present facilities weren't able to handle all the sick and infirm who came her way.

The leader of the group then asked, "Dr. Campolo, would you please lead us in prayer that the Lord might provide the five thousand dollars that is needed by our sister in Venezuela?"

Before I could catch myself I said, "No, but what I will do is take all the money I am carrying on me and put it on the altar. Then I'm going to ask everyone else here to do the same. No need to write out checks! We'll only accept cash! After we've all put the cash we're carrying on the altar, we'll count it. If we don't have five thousand dollars, I'll ask God to write out a check for the difference."

It was a good day to pull this off, because I was only carrying $2.25. The leader smiled benevolently and said, "We've all gotten the point, haven't we?"

I responded, "No! I don't think we have! My $2.25 is on the altar. Now it's your turn!"

She was somewhat taken aback by my aggressive request, but she opened her wallet and pulled out $110 and slapped it down on top of my meager offering. Then I said, "We're on our way! We've got $112.25. Now it's your turn!"

I pointed to a woman who was sitting in the front pew over to my right. She looked around and smiled a bit. Then she got up and came to the altar and put her cash on top of ours. I got the next woman to do it, then the next, and the next. It took me more than twenty-five minutes to take up the offering as one by one, woman after woman came and placed her money on the communion table. When they had finished taking turns laying their money on the altar, we counted it. We had taken in more than eight thousand dollars. Even then, I knew I hadn't gotten all of the cash. I could see some of the women putting in meager offerings, holding back most of what they had, and giving me dirty looks.

There wasn't any time left for me to preach. I don't think they wanted to hear from me anyway, so I simply said to the congregation, "The audacity of asking God for five thousand dollars, when He has already provided us with more than eight thousand dollars. We should not be asking God to supply our needs. *He already has!*"

The Christians in the early church did not have to be manipulated into giving as I did with those women. We read in II Corinthians 8:3b-4, "they voluntarily gave according to their means, and even beyond their means, begging us earnestly for the privilege of sharing in this ministry to the saints." Those first century Christians were motivated out of love for others and out of gratitude to God for the salvation that was available through Christ, to give sacrificially. This is not the case among most Christians today, and that is the reason that we have resorted to fund raising that utilizes the techniques of Madison Avenue and from professional fund raisers of the secular society.

It has been said: "The medium is the message." The *ways* in which we communicate really tells people what we are all about, much more than the words we employ. This is especially true when it comes to conveying to church members what is required of them in stewardship. When we employ methodologies for fund raising that ignore biblical prescriptions we divert people from what Christian stewardship is all about.

This book is a call to reconsider stewardship as the core of discipleship and spells out how we can recover ministering by giving in ways that honor God.

TONY CAMPOLO, Ph.D.
Professor Emeritus
Eastern University
St. Davids, PA

Acknowledgments

My values about stewardship are most fundamentally rooted in my faith, but were deepened and enhanced by the opportunity for religious and theological education. I am also grateful for my experience as a parish Development Officer in the Roman Catholic Church in the Archdiocese of New York, as well as my work with Anglican, Roman Catholic, United Church (Methodist/ Presbyterian), Evangelical and Jewish communities in the United States and Canada. Taken together, these have had a profound impact on my practical ideas concerning philanthropy and Christian stewardship. Without the privilege of working with these faith communities, I would not have been able to offer these insights with any sense of authority or assurance. I am indebted to everyone who invited me in to this breadth of experience, and trust that my demonstrated success with them over the years has been of equal value to them.

Following the urging of many of the people and in congregations across Canada and the United States with whom I have worked, I have decided to share my research and experience in the hope of assisting the Church, its clergy, laity, and especially those who are called upon to provide expertise in Christian stewardship, to come to a healthier understanding of good stewardship practices, and to embrace the "more excellent way" of vocational stewardship. I hope that each reader of this book might embrace the theology of abundance more fully, and so develop both themselves and the Church to be the passionate stewards for whom God created us in his image—joyful, gifted and unceasingly generous.

Deciding to write this book was very difficult. Ultimately, it meant challenging many "traditional" thoughts and views that underlie the conventional wisdom about stewardship. In so doing, I risk alienating people who were trained in outmoded "process driven" and "legalistic" approaches to stewardship. Moreover, many of the leaders in the Church, especially those with responsibilities at the denominational level, were not only "raised" in the traditions which I challenge, but in many cases serve in decision-making positions that determine how stewardship and fundraising are administered for their conference/denomination. While I have no desire to offend those who have in the past approved and adopted the methods and ideas which this book challenges, I felt an obligation to set forth a "more excellent way," and to *re*-commend to the Church an approach to stewardship which is not only empirically and theologically defensible, but which is more fully in keeping with our vocation as Christians.

I would also like to thank, in no particular order, those who most encouraged me in my work, especially the people, organizations and faith communities who have provided me with the experience and professional support to undertake this book: the International Catholic Stewardship Council; The Episcopal Network for Stewardship; the Canadian Centre for Philanthropy; the Canadian Association of Gift Planners; the Urban Institute's National Center for Charitable Statistics; the Reverend Canon Philip Poole; the Most Reverend Edward W. Scott; Friars of the Atonement The Reverends Pascal Breaux, S.A., and Damian MacPherson, S.A.; Audrey Dorsch, Pastor Bill Page and the entire congregation of Bethel Evangelical Missionary Church and all others who helped make this book possible.

And a special note of gratitude to Barbara Newman, M.D., a fine physician and inspiration to all who know her.

I would be remiss if I did not mention my wife, The Reverend Canon M. Ansley Tucker, M.Div., Th.M., whose constant support and encouragement gave me the courage and inspiration to write this book. Her willingness to offer constructive criticism and argue specific points (in the finest tradition of academic pursuit) helped me to continually refine my thoughts and writing—not to mention engage in the constructive theological and philosophical debates which have come to be a sign of our ecumenical marriage. Without her steadfast convictions, unparalleled integrity, and devotion to the Church, I would not have had the courage to challenge conventional wisdom, and take my stand with a handful of leaders in North America who also long for the Church to recover stewardship in its orthodox, historic and vocational sense. I count myself blessed to be numbered amongst them.

Most of all, I am eternally indebted to God, from whom all good things come!

Prologue

Writing a book on Christian stewardship that will serve all who confess Jesus requires a great deal of ecumenical sensitivity. In the first printing of this book, meant for the Roman Catholic and Anglican communities, for the sake of clarity, I attempted to use the most universal and inclusive terms possible. The task was not always easy, as the divisions in the Christian community have given rise to unique vocabularies and practices amongst its different confessions and traditions. In the end, I did not think that this spoke meaningfully enough to my brothers and sisters in the evangelical community.

Consequently, I am now pleased to release this revised edition addressed specifically to the broad evangelical body of the Christian Church. Even that tradition, I must recognize, does not have homogenous vocabularies and practices. However, I trust that my attempt, as well as the efforts of my co-publisher, to address this broad sector with a single volume will be accepted as a genuine desire to overcome the barriers of Babel so that Christ's Kingdom may benefit.

The vocabulary with which people speak about stewardship and their varied definitions of the word are as multitudinous as the churches and ecclesial communities that have arisen from the Christian confession of faith. Over the two millennia of Christian history, Western Civilization has gone through many changes, and the churches with it. Emerging from a persecuted community who worshiped in the catacombs, once the Church was united with the

State it became incorporated in a society that has made the transition from sacral to pluralist, and now to secular.

From the moment the Roman Emperor Constantine was victorious at the Milvian Bridge in 312 C.E., and established Christianity as the official religion of the empire, the Church's understanding of stewardship has been propelled along a course of change that the Apostles could not have imagined. Once the Church ceased to be a persecuted minority, and was embraced not only by society, but by the governing authority, our understanding of Christian stewardship, and the related traditions which had developed in the early Church, became mediated not by theology and reason, but by forces which were not always consistent with the radical newness of the Christian message.

By the middle ages, the worldly enrichment that went hand in hand with religious fundraising created a *causa belli* amongst many of the faithful, leading in part to the Protestant Reformation. Alongside his theological complaints, Martin Luther specifically condemned the Church's fundraising practices, and especially the sale of indulgences.[1] Nevertheless, unworthy stewardship practices were not routed by the Reformation. As Lutherans found favor in their princes, and later the English Reformation in their King and Queens, despite their best efforts, churches remained inescapably tied to the State; not surprisingly, some of the same ills that had at times led to corruption in the Roman Catholic Church quickly left their mark on the new Protestant churches, and the states where they were established.

---

[1] "Disputation Of Doctor Martin Luther On The Power And Efficacy Of Indulgences," October 31, 1517, No. 86: "Again:—Why does not the pope, whose wealth is to-day greater than the riches of the richest, build just this one church of St. Peter with his own money, rather than with the money of poor believers?" In *Works of Doctor Martin Luther*, ed. and trans. Adolph Spaeth *et al.*, vol. 1 (Philadelphia: A. J. Holman Co., 1915), pp. 29–38.

The emergence of plural ecclesiastic communities operating separately, but still alongside the State, began to force these new faith communities, as well as the traditional mainline churches, to a position of self-reliance, and financial independence. Not until religious tolerance (and therefore pluralism) really took hold during Europe's Enlightenment, an expression that reached its zenith in the colonies that would become the United States, did government commence in earnest a determined policy of abolishing the Church-State relationship. This abolition (not necessarily to say prohibition) of a Church-State relationship necessitated a reconsideration of how churches and their charitable works would be financed, leading to the first real review of fundraising and stewardship practices since the Apostolic era. In many ways, we are recovering stewardship not from a secularism dating to the age of Enlightenment, but from State influence and secularism dating back to the reign of Constantine the Great in the fourth Century.

For these reasons, and given the variations in the theological language of our several ecclesial communities, it is exceedingly difficult to speak about stewardship using a common lexicon. The "scandal of division" to which Pope John XXIII referred rests not only upon theological foundations, but upon practice, tradition and language. It is my hope that we can focus on the first principles of stewardship which, while described uniquely in the governing documents of the local church, conference or denomination, still hold an amazing fidelity to the orthodoxy of the New Testament church.

A book of this type inevitably attracts detractors who argue with the source of the statistics cited, the methodology by which they have been gathered, and other technical matters in this vein. I can only say that I have tried to use responsible sources for statistical data. However, there are few organizations that gather such data pertaining to philanthropy, especially religious philanthropy.

The head of a research department for a leading national "think tank" on philanthropy described the collection of philanthropic data as akin to sausage making, "… you never know what goes in and once it's wrapped you don't want to ask." I do not think things to be all that bad, but there are certain concerns I and others share about the reliability of what data is generally available. While I reserve my concerns about the specific reliability of certain figures, I have generally found that the institutions which collect the type of data I have cited in this book uniformly agree about the basic trends I have sought to elucidate.

Finally, I would like to add a note about points of sensitivity. Throughout the text I have chosen to use the designation C.E. (Common Era) for historic dating. This was done in deference to our Orthodox and Eastern Rite brothers and sisters who keep a different calendar, as well as our elder brothers and sisters in faith, the Jewish People, whose calendar was not fixed until 359 C.E. by Sanhedrin president Hillel II.

Chapter I
An Introduction to Stewardship

The Faithful Steward: Reclaiming Stewardship for Christ's Kingdom is not a "how to" manual; it is not an exegesis of pertinent scriptural passages; nor is it a handbook for program implementation. This work is primarily concerned with naming the current crisis in Christian stewardship, identifying its underlying causes, elucidating the ways in which we have lost touch with the fundamental wisdom of Christianity, and suggesting a way forward which is in keeping with our Christian faith and ancient history. In this sense, this work is a "why to" treatment of Christian stewardship for the Christian churches and organizations today. Only once we have dealt with first principles can we properly turn to questions of method and practice, issues for a more in-depth treatment in a different publication.

As attendance in the historic, mainline churches declines across North America, congregations are getting smaller, slowly shrinking with the diminished importance of religion to society, reduced to an aging remnant who fondly recall "the good 'ole days" as depicted in Norman Rockwell's paintings of religious America. With the dwindling size of congregations, and the continued planting of new congregations, it is not surprising that these mainline churches are stretching their clergy and lay volunteers in ministry thin. Many report being overburdened to the point that they are unable to fulfill their commitment to their church in a manner which also meets the legitimate demands of family, work and friends, thereby forcing people to choose between church (not faith, mind you) and family.

Even some evangelical circles face a shortage of pastors in many critical areas, leading them to ask lay ministers to take on an increasing amount of work, while their pay continues to fall behind the average earned income, with no increase in available time. The one constant that cannot be changed is the 24-hour day and the 7-day week.

When churches were part of a generally Christian society, people professed to be more theistic, looking to their church for guidance and wisdom in the management of their everyday affairs. The churches' practices were in this sense exemplary, and were actually considered modern in their age. But religious pluralism has forced society and religion apart over the past few centuries. Society, having completed the transition from religious, to pluralist, and now reaching a state of secularism, has led many people to believe that the churches' values, convictions and teachings are simply benign, quaint or just plain irrelevant.

From time to time, a blip appears on the radar screen, and it seems as if this trend might be in reversal. In the aftermath of the terrorist attacks of September 11, 2001, for example, it was captivating to watch an apparent reintegration of government and society with the churches (except in Canada where the official commemoration ceremonies on September 15 "for Canadians on Parliament Hill made no reference to any of the religious traditions to which the majority of Canadians turn in their own times of grief and loss").[2] Only months later, however, it was evident that this

---

[2] Archbishop Michael Peers (Primate of the Anglican Church of Canada), "My Canada Includes God," *The Globe & Mail,* 16 March 2002, p. A17. Also, in the aftermath of the loss of Swissair Flight 111 off of Peggy's Cove, Nova Scotia, the Canadian government prohibited Christian clerics from invoking the name of Jesus in their prayers for the lost souls and their grieving family members, friends and loved ones.

mutual embrace was short-lived. Those who made their way back to the Church just as quickly left again, thereby returning the churches to a steady and long-standing decline in significance to society at large. Secular society and religion seem consigned to share a common, yet separate, existence.

The struggle then becomes how each exists in the balance. Does Christianity pursue a less traditional and "organized" approach to life, and therefore reflect the current secular desire for individualism? Does Christianity re-engage in its core teachings, calling society to become part of the Church—the Body of Christ? Or does Christianity walk a tightrope, balancing each of these and other perspectives as an acrobat walks the high wire? These are far-reaching questions: our intent here is to deal with them only in so far as they pertain to Christian stewardship.

My contention is that ancient as the churches' ideas may be, they are, and continue to be, timeless. However, in the ill-conceived attempt to prove themselves to society at large, the churches have relinquished some of their most important teachings and practices about stewardship. Over the years the churches have embraced secular fundraising practices instead of asserting and commending the fuller principles of *stewardship* to society. In doing so, stewardship was reduced to giving—and not only giving, but mere financial giving. In trying to integrate what is perceived as the success of secular fundraising, Christian stewardship was all but abandoned. Indeed, the idea of stewardship has come to be more associated with the environmental lobby than the churches.

"Fundraising" is all about non-profit management practices, and goals which are quantifiable and therefore, measurable. Consequently, fundraising does not concern itself with faith and grace, both of which defy quantification and methodical implementation. Moreover, whatever values are at the heart of secular fundraising have been reduced to a donor-centered "Donor Bill of Rights," instead of focusing on the recipients of such gifts in accordance with the true reason for fundraising—philanthropy, which derives its meaning from the ancient Greek, *philia* (meaning love) and *anthropos* (meaning humanity).

Stewardship, by contrast, is a matter of living out our vocation as Christians. The values which underlie Christian stewardship are not grounded in the Enlightenment's sense of individual rights, but in the idea of gratitude to our Creator, Redeemer and Sustainer, and the inherent dignity which belongs to every human being, and which at times requires the assistance of others.

This book is not a condemnation of secular fundraising; this is not its purpose. It is, however, a condemnation of how secular fundraising practices and values have corrupted and disfigured the image of generosity and love that are at the heart of Christian stewardship. Although secular fundraising models and practices may be appropriate for colleges, universities, libraries and other secular non-profit organizations, they are not suitable for the Christian churches and organizations, for the very reason that they fundamentally undermine the Christian values we profess individually and communally. Secular fundraising deprives us of our ability to give witness to our faith. In employing its methods, we at times give "counter-witness" to the Gospel, as will be made evident in this book.

One of the first principles of stewardship is that we give, give generously, and give without expectation of praise and/or compensation. This runs counter to most secular practices of donor recognition, where donors are continuously honored, recognized and given "premiums" in the hopes of "cultivating" them to give again. The secular expectation of receiving something in return has even crept into the rituals of Christmas, where gifts are more often "exchanged" than given.

We must learn to give without expectation of return. Imagine what church members would say if a minister took to the pulpit and offered a nice tote bag to anyone who would give at the $50 level. And while those who endow libraries and hospitals may rightly expect to have a building named for themselves or their family, can you imagine what it would be like to have one of its members or adherents, a major donor to the church, ask to have the First Street Baptist Church renamed *"The Smith Family Church"*? Giving and generosity are not transactional—they are vocational, and therefore should not need the encouragement of donor recognition schemes and trinkets.

As part of its everyday work, secular fundraising employs these recognition and premium programs as well as other practices designed to *induce* giving. Over the past fifty years Christian churches and organizations to a greater or lesser extent have done likewise when they adopted these practices in their efforts to help finance their ministries. I believe that by employing secular fundraising practices we have been more concerned with outcomes than values, method than theology, and major gifts than generosity. This being said, there is nothing to be gained by assigning blame and revisiting the past, except to learn from our mistakes.

We should start by naming the secular fundraising practices that have crept into our personal and communal values, and identifying how they affect our Christian vocation as stewards. If we have embraced the hard-nosed practices of secular fundraising out of fear of becoming less important to society at large, or of standing up to the often insurmountable pressures of secularism, we need to ask ourselves what we can do about it. We must have the confessional will, moral courage, and fortitude, to acknowledge that we have gone off track, and to reform our practices to reflect our faith and values.

We can begin by examining whether and how we have provided for the education of our leadership and members in issues of stewardship. While our seminaries and Bible colleges have quite rightly concerned themselves with biblical studies, pastoral care, liturgical practice and church history, they have generally failed to take seriously the issue of stewardship. Few, if any, institutions in the theological academy have adequate academic or practical training and education in the areas of money, financial management, volunteer administration, and the finer principles of congregational stewardship development.

When we fail to educate our teachers and leaders in these areas, we should not be surprised that the faithful are equally ill formed and informed. Indeed, if stewardship education is inadequate for pastors, it is all but non-existent for the members. Much of what has been embraced by Christian churches and organizations emulates what has been seen as "successful" in secular terms, most often expressed in terms of the number of dollars raised. Most lay people who undertake leadership roles in the stewardship ministry of their church or organization—through no fault of their own—generally received what little training they have from secular fundraising firms, and non-profit education seminars. Few if any of these programs are concerned with community, fewer with education and personal development, and fewer yet with theology. If we truly value stewardship we must rediscover our own understanding of stewardship, begin to teach it, teach it often, and teach it well.

Few denominations provide much professional and spiritual development for their stewardship teachers and leaders at the national and international levels. Indeed, participation in these organizations, and their professional development and education programs, varies widely. While it is true that Methodists and some other communities in the United States have "regional" bodies to assist in the area of stewardship, most Christian churches and organizations too often rely upon an over-worked, under-experienced, and under-funded denominational to meet the needs of their ministries. (This may very well be a reflection of how each of these religious communities embraces the idea of governance, and not a disregard for appropriate development.)

In theory, these stewardship officers are hired generally to support all of the denominational stewardship efforts within their geographic region. In reality, however, by the time most denominational stewardship officers perform the work required for the appeals they administer, attend national and regional conference functions, support planned giving initiatives, meet with their fellow staff members and attend to their own professional and spiritual development, there is virtually no time left to spend with congregations.

Even when denominational stewardship officers, ministers and other lay leaders have thorough training and knowledge in appropriate Christian stewardship, the ease of implementing a "cookie-cutter," secular method or approach to fundraising becomes increasingly appealing in the face of time, staffing and other resource constraints. These dynamics only exacerbate the propensity of secular fundraising methods and practices to supplant real Christian stewardship. And when internal time and resource constraints do not allow for denominational stewardship officers to work with all of their congregations and organizations, there is a tendency to "augment" the staff by hiring outside consultants, almost all of whom conduct a mix of secular and religious fundraising. Given the relative inability of most conferences and denominations to serve their congregations internally, secular fundraisers who, at best, run "church departments," become surrogate stewardship officers, held out to be experts, despite in most cases a fundamental lack of theological or religious development.[3]

Consequently, ministers and other leaders use secular fundraisers, adopting their "expertise," language, and practices—

---

[3] It is common practice amongst fundraising firms to promise Churches the "expertise and supervision of senior staff" while employing young, inexperienced and/or untrained staff to conduct the campaign as "on site" counsel. The founder of a firm that has in the past conducted the majority of large Church fundraising campaigns in Canada once said to me, "I always send a new fundraiser to learn their work in the Church. If they mess up there, the Church will always forgive them, while a hospital or a school will cancel their contract."

further alienating stewardship from its true status and role in the lives of the faithful. Simply put, a variety of causal factors has created an environment where few ministers or the faithful any longer understand or embrace the true nature of Christian stewardship.

To better understand stewardship I believe it necessary to make an affirmative statement about what it is. Consider the following classical descriptions of Christian stewardship:

- Stewardship is the proper and generous use of our time, talent and treasure.
- Stewardship is all that we do with our lives after we profess our faith.
- Stewardship is about joyfully returning to God a portion of that bounty which God has bestowed upon us.
- Stewardship is about gratuitously sharing with Christ's Body (Rm 12:3-8), all the gifts that God has entrusted to us.

These are working definitions from which we can proceed. But to employ St. Thomas Aquinas' style of argumentation, I think it equally useful to approach stewardship from a *via negativa* perspective, or more clearly, to examine what it is *not*.

Experience suggests that the following are some of the more common ideas about what stewardship is not. Stewardship is not just about duty, responsibility, or financial giving. Stewardship is not about who gives most, or who can give enough to be considered for "naming opportunities." Neither is stewardship disconnected from how we live as Christians. Stewardship is not about giving time without treasure; treasure without talent; talent without time; nor any other combination: it is rather, the triune and complete use of all three of these aspects—our life—for the glory of God.

Stewardship is so intrinsically part of our vocation as Christians that we cannot place it above or below prayer—but essentially with it. Our acts of charity can be a prayer for humanity. We give in gratitude, and therefore praise God. It can even be argued that our vocation as Christians is based in our faith, and lived out (expressed) through our acts of stewardship. A good steward is mindful of time, talent, and treasure, and uses all three to engage in prayer, worship, acts of charity, mercy, kindness, humility, and love, sustaining them all by embracing stewardship.

The churches, and the society in which we live, are increasingly showing signs of alienation from these classical ideas of stewardship. Resources are no longer seen as precious gifts from God with which we have been entrusted, but as assets by which profit might be gained or the institution protected. While there is nothing wrong with profit *per se,* unwholesome profit belies our vocation as stewards, be we sellers or consumers.

The notion of biblical stewardship obviates the distinction between wealth and poverty. What matters is generosity. A good steward understands his or her wealth *as gift* and shares it proportionately. This means that even the poorest of the poor can be a good steward. The small gift of a pauper may be vastly more generous than the large gift of a rich person. Like the widow with the mite that was "all she had to live on" (Mk 12:41–44), godly stewards are impelled to give from the well of their deep desire. Secular stewards, by contrast, are more concerned with the dollar amount, recognition, and what might be gained in return for their "gift."

I often wonder if St. Francis of Assisi, himself a lover of the scriptures, and modest living, when contemplating the bounty of God's love and generosity in a very troubled world, might not have committed to prayer something like this:

> God, make me a steward of your bounty.
> Where there is need, let me see it;
> Where there is abundance, let me share it;
> Where there is time, let me spend it;
> and where there is treasure, let me use it to your glory!

The recovery of good stewardship from secular fundraising will not be the immediate panacea to the ills of churches and society, but it will be crucial if we are to liberate the resources at our disposal for the work for which Christian ministries and churches have been instituted and called. It is not enough for Christian churches and organizations simply to "keep on keeping on." We need to permit ourselves to dream, to surpass the status quo, and to ask what we could and should be doing. To realize our deepest vocation we will surely need to develop ourselves as stewards. Indeed, while the gifts we give will never save us, our acts of stewardship, in so far as they are in keeping with God's plan for humanity, do offer us the dignity of participating in God's plan of redemption.

Stewardship is not the by-product of a committee meeting or a fundraising campaign, nor even of the Sunday sermon. Stewardship is a relationship with God that both receives and gives, making all things possible. Christian stewards recognize their gifts, contemplate all that is in their lives, and devote themselves daily to the conviction that they, as Christians, are invited into a state of duality: as a child of God, the Christian is *gift*, and as steward, *giver*. Life as a steward, contained in the covenant of our profession of faith, and embodied in the daily journey of our lives, is intrinsic to Christian discipleship.

Christian communities, including conferences, denominations, presbyteries, synods, and other organizations, need to understand that the recovery of Christian stewardship from secular fundraising is vital to the life of our Christian communities. It seems a paradox that we must reach into our antiquity, to the teachings and practices of the New Testament communities, and even back to Judaic wisdom and history, if we are to return stewardship to its proper place in our contemporary life. But only thus—by faith, God's grace, and good stewardship—can we hope to reach out to where God always calls us, and society expects us to serve.

God not only calls us to quit what is wrong, but to do what is right. In this sense, stewardship is not passive, but is by definition inherently active. To become "the passionate steward" requires positive acts, both personally and communally. We must reform in accordance with the prophetic voice of Isaiah who says, in respect of our conduct, and of the vulnerable that we are to serve with dignity:

Cease to do evil, learn to do good! Seek justice, rescue the oppressed. Defend the orphan, plead for the widow (Is 1:16–17).

Chapter II
Professing our Christian Vocation – Embracing our Lives as Stewards

As Christians, we are used to making proclamations about the nature and content of our vocation. Being a Christian, we say, calls us to struggle for justice. It calls us to forgive others. It calls us, as part of our very vocation, to be passionate stewards.

Stewardship, however, is not a vocation that stands independently, but rather, as part of our greater vocation as Christians. Stewardship cannot, therefore, be achieved in singular acts of giving, but instead through the total conduct of our lives as followers of Christ. Like Christian life itself, stewardship is a journey. It takes time, we stumble, we fall, and we rise again to pursue our Christian vocation. We progress as stewards even as we progress as pilgrims. In this sense, we grow after the example of Christ who matured "in wisdom and in years, and in divine and human favor" (Lk 2:52). Christ, in his generous self-sacrifice, sets before us the perfection of loving self-donation. He is the Passionate Steward—the model we are called to imitate.

Doubtless, our journey as stewards, much like Christ's journey, will be punctuated by particular milestones—moments of sacrifice or special generosity which will stand out always in our lives, or perhaps of learning or insight which "form" us as stewards. Perhaps a Sunday school teacher will encourage in us an indelible desire to share, or to deepen our sense of gratitude for blessings we have not earned. As adults, we may find ourselves moved by a sermon, enriched by the gift of our time and talent as volunteers, or changed by our participation in a special collection or capital campaign. With each of these experiences we learn, and yet, none of them can ever represent the full attainment of our vocation to stewardship whereby we seek to emulate Christ in the totality of his self-offering sacrifice of salvation.

Here is why. Good stewardship is not predicated on a single act. No vocation is. While the act of ordination may make someone a minister, for example, we would not consider this a fulfillment of that person's vocation, but rather a single milestone in living out his or her life "as servant." Nor can we achieve the fullness of our vocation as good stewards by a single act of generosity. Indeed, it most often works the other way round: being a good steward is what compels us to a life filled with singular acts of generosity.

As our lives evolve, then, so should our understanding and practice of stewardship. Just as we pray to deepen our faith, or to better understand what God calls us to be in life, so we must also continually work to discern our vocation as stewards. Anyone who has engaged in the life of prayer knows that the more we pray, the deeper our prayer life becomes. The stewardship journey is no different: the more deeply we engage in it, the better we understand it, and the better we understand it, the more richly we are called to participate in the redemptive ministry of Jesus Christ.

The essence of stewardship is that it transcends the cumulative learning and experience of its various milestones. That is, it is more than the sum of its parts. Hence, signal moments in our journey as stewards serve not merely to edify us, but are transformative. Our understanding of stewardship—personal, corporate, or observed—is worthless unless we actually put the *idea* of stewardship into *action* in our daily lives. In this sense stewardship falls within the scope of Aristotle's *Metaphysics*: it goes beyond the physical, changing our hearts, rekindling not only our understanding, but also the very expression of our human essence—so that by being a passionate steward, we who *are* good, *do* good.

The passionate steward *desires* to be generous with his or her time, talent and treasure, and therefore *acts* upon that desire. Motivated by an understanding of one's Christian vocation as a steward, the individual Christian gives, gives generously, gives freely, and gives without expectation of reward or recognition. For the passionate steward such a gift conforms to the norms of Scripture. It is an act of love, freedom and generosity—not an act of obligation, duty, or social expectation.

However, because of the way Christian ministries and congregations have approached stewardship in recent decades many Christians have come to think of stewardship as something transitory and transactional. Rather than according stewardship its rightful place in our ongoing life and preaching, we have relegated it to points of intense, but time-limited focus, such as special campaigns, foundation appeals, and the establishment of endowment funds. In other words, the milestones have been permitted to substitute for the journey.

Accordingly, members' interest is piqued only during such campaigns themselves, and the life-changing nature of Christian stewardship is lost. The result is that the congregation becomes even more deeply reliant upon the aforementioned secular models to provide for mission and ministry. This practice thus becomes cyclical: the more the congregation relies upon special efforts and less on stewardship, the less it will experience stewardship, and the more often it will have to administer campaigns.

It is no wonder that members often complain that the congregation or the denomination "always has its hand out." We spend a disproportionate amount of our time, talent and treasure seeking time, talent and treasure—simply because we teach secular fundraising, not stewardship. Unless we as Christians resolve to change this pattern we will be bound to repeat it until we expend so much of our energy fundraising, that liturgy, worship, education, outreach, and other ministries lose their place as our primary Christian focus.

To be sure, over the past half-century, secular fundraising organizations have helped the Christian ministries to raise untold amounts of money. The bricks and mortar of thousands of churches are testimony to their assistance. But just as their success in raising money is etched in plaques on church walls, the model of giving they have taught is engraved on the hearts of the faithful. In my ministry of teaching stewardship and assisting churches to raise millions of dollars, I have often had to deal with the deep impression secular fundraisers have left upon the members, even decades after their experience of a previous campaign. What secular fundraisers teach as appropriate models of giving and "stewardship" have become so ingrained in the minds of the members, that any attempt to present a higher and more Christian understanding of stewardship is very often greeted with disdain and condemnation.

Part of our difficulty is that we have so imbibed secular models, and so thoroughly integrated them into our language, life and practice, that to set them aside will require us first to admit that there are some things about which we were quite simply wrong.

At the heart of our difficulty are a fundamentally utilitarian philosophy and a commercial culture about money. Some argue, "Secular fundraising works, so why mess with success?" "Secular fundraisers," I have been told, "raise more money than the churches ever have on their own. Why wouldn't we want to do what they do?"

The overarching problem is that secular fundraisers are focused primarily on quantifiable—that is to say, *financial*—results, whereas the congregation must concern itself not only with measures of quantity, but with the *quality* of its communal life, and the motivations and attitudes with which its members lay *all* their gifts (not just their money) before God. To focus on the size of a gift, without reference to generosity and charitable intent, let alone time and talent, is to vitiate the richness of true Christian stewardship.

Having embraced secular fundraising for so long, we should not be surprised that it has disfigured the image of Christian stewardship. A key failing of secular models is that they normally focus on the *method* by which to get people to give rather than on their *motivation* for doing so (as is most appropriate for the congregation). Most secular fundraisers, for example, use the "gift chart" method, whereby members are sorted or "segmented" according to their monetary value to the congregation. Such campaigns are based upon the premise that to achieve a certain financial goal, an organization must "target" a few people to give "lead gifts" in advance of the campaign in order to encourage others to give; a few more are solicited for "major gifts" of a predetermined level, in order to demonstrate that others should also be motivated to make large gifts; still others are targeted for "pace setting gifts,"—all in the attempt to ensure that the congregation has met particular financial milestones before issuing the call for "general giving" from everyone else (who are by far the majority of possible donors). Despite such practices undercutting some of our most basic Christian values, many churches have followed suit. Some stewardship officers who serve at the denominational level actually publish such charts to help congregations determine whether they can raise the money they need. In this case congregations, including their pastors and board leadership, assume that the "experts" at the denominational level know what they are doing, and unquestioningly adopt those practices and methods as models of "good stewardship."

Another tool invariably used by secular fundraisers is the donor recognition incentive. For a princely sum, one can be memorialized in a wall plaque; for a less princely sum, one receives membership in the "Preacher's Circle;" and for a suitably sizable contribution you can receive an invitation to dine with the bishop, moderator or other similar church leader, and other wealthy donors of record. This is not stewardship. It is the marketing of recognition. Any tactic intended to instigate or reward giving nullifies the act as *gift* and reduces it to *transaction* (Mt 6:1-4). And yet churches uncritically adopt such practices as the means to successful fundraising.

Demonstrating our appreciation for generosity should not be tied to reward, but should flow from the inherent gratitude with which one accepts a gift. The very idea of generosity hinging upon donor recognition is undercut by the example of the poor widow Jesus noticed dropping a worthless coin into the alms box (Mk 12:41–44). It was all she had to live on, but if Jesus hadn't been looking, would anyone even have known she gave it, let alone thanked her? And yet hers is the gift which Jesus held up as an example of true stewardship.

When attending conferences, speaking to denominational bodies, or discussing stewardship with my professional peers, I often struggle to make the point that stewardship is not method-driven. Good stewardship, whether exercised corporately by the congregation as a whole, or individually by each Christian, cannot be achieved simply by following the instructions in a "how to" book we pick up at our local Christian bookstore. Such books can certainly help with issues of administration and organization, but they are wholly inadequate when it comes to teaching good stewardship. Good stewardship stems from our fundamental understanding of the radical values of the Gospel, and from that faith in God which together motivate our desire to return generosity for abundance.

In many ways, Canadian Marshall McLuhan's declaration that "the medium is the message" could not be more clearly illustrated. If popular secular practices such as emphasizing large gifts and offering donor recognition are the medium by which we raise money, then the message is that to give freely and joyfully of our time, talent and treasure is unimportant—what we pray and do becomes the witness to our faith. God save us from an approach to stewardship which makes an idol of money or greed.

Secular models of fundraising simply do not teach stewardship, and are almost always contrary to our confessions and values. Stewardship considers the soul. Secular fundraising does not. Our growth into passionate stewards is about *inward change* for *outward action* throughout our lives. Secular fundraising, by contrast, has a definite *telos*—its primary focus is an ordered end, a destination, generally quantified in financial terms only. For a Christian, a fundraising campaign can never be more than a milestone in one's lifelong journey, while for secular fundraisers, a gift can be the completion of one's philanthropic goals.

The congregation needs to recover its first principles. We cannot simply surrender to secular methods because they seem to "work," or because they have kept us from the brink of bankruptcy before. Stewardship is not about sending the right person to ask for the gift, nor is it about dangling donor recognition and sycophantic praise in front of members in the hopes of prying open their purse. What is at stake here is nothing less than our Christian values, and our faith in the Gospel itself. We are mistaken if we believe that when it comes to money, and when money is what pays the bills, we have little choice but to jettison our Christian convictions.

In the wake of the current scandals concerning the sexual abuse of young men and women, and the not too distantly past scandals of many high level televangelists, many churches will find themselves lost if they continue to rely upon providing reasons and tools to induce people to give. For example, in April 2002, The New York Times declared that the Roman Catholic Archdiocese of Boston was in critical financial trouble because people had stopped putting money in the collection plate to protest the way Cardinal Law had handled cases of abuse. While it is understandable that grief may lead people to imprudent acts, it is necessary to wonder if a well developed steward would ever withhold gifts to God because of human sin. Sadly, with the current trend to see giving through the lens of a "Donor Bill of Rights" it is understandable how a donor could withhold an offering for political gain or cause. Do not think that the scandals of sexual abuse are limited to the mainline churches. From Jim and Tammy Baker to Cardinal Law, the message is clear—no person or congregation is immune from sin and its affect on them personally and amongst the leadership and the faithful.

Once *stewards* learn to think of themselves as mere *donors*, and of their money as leverage, it is a short step to the erosion of our ability to continue to provide for ministry, feed the hungry, clothe the poor, and shelter the homeless. Depriving the congregation of one's gifts only exacerbates the problem: the congregation is now guilty not only of misconduct, but of failing to fulfill its mission—which, according to the commandment given through Isaiah, is to care for the poor, the widow and the orphan.

How we emerge from this state will say much about our values and character as a community of faith. Our future depends not upon treating our financial problems like ciphers to be solved, or seeing congregation members through a utilitarian lens as the answer to our financial problems. We must help every individual Christian understand and embrace the idea that our vocation *calls* us to give, give freely, give generously, and most importantly, to give joyfully in praise of God, and in support of the congregation which continues to preach the Gospel, and strives to turn away from evil to do good.

Should we continue to embrace those secular fundraising practices which have taken root in our house, our credibility will only continue to decline amongst the faithful. For example, in the context of the Christian community's criticism of high interest rates and of personal debt as oppressive to the security of the average family, many churches have simultaneously adopted such debt-making practices as encouraging members to make pledge payments using their credit cards. We risk alienating even the most steadfast amongst the faithful when we do not embrace our own teachings.

A report by the Canadian Centre for Philanthropy only confirms what those of us who desire a recovery of good stewardship principles and practices have said for years—"some fundraising practices used by Canadian charities may be at odds with public expectations."[4] The same practices that Canadians find incompatible are equally offensive to Americans. People throughout North America increasingly indicate that they are wearying of progressively more sophisticated fundraising practices. The problem has reached such proportions that donors are beginning to complain to legislative bodies about the amount of research being conducted into their backgrounds in the pursuit of larger and larger major gifts. It is the mission of Christian organizations to demonstrate and give witness to our faith and values. We must, in the end, practice what we preach.

---

[4] Michael Hall, *Charitable Fundraising in Canada: Results from a National Survey of Fundraising Practices of Canadian Charities* (Toronto: The Canadian Centre for Philanthropy, 1996), p. 41.

Chapter III
Challenging Conventional Wisdom about Religious Giving

In my work as a development officer and now as a "professional" stewardship and fundraising consultant I am constantly asked, "Why don't people give?" or "Why don't people give more?" To answer these questions we need to dissect the issue of charitable giving in North America, and in particular, religious giving.

My response to the first question, "Why don't people give?" is simple—they do! To be sure, there are certain trends in the manner and motivation of charitable giving which are sufficient to give pause, and these need to be examined. Further, as noted, many churches have uncritically adopted the practices and assumptions inherent in secular models of fundraising, often without realizing that we have been seduced by assumptions which run counter to biblical teaching. This has given rise to a body of "conventional wisdom" which may be neither all that wise, nor conventional. Challenging our assumptions about how and why people give, however, is essential to understanding how we can recover stewardship from secular fundraising.

Most people assume that Jesus' proclamation, "Where your treasure is, there your heart will be also" (Mt 6:21) means that the hearts of the faithful follow their purse strings. Reason and experience suggest a far more profound truth. When we view treasure as encompassing more than money, we can imagine it signifying different things to different people. Like many busy North Americans living in a hectic and demanding society, my greatest treasure is not my money, which I can replace through the years with future earnings, but my time—which once spent, generally survives only in memory, unless invested in people where it will live on in their thoughts, deeds and dreams. Time is therefore an extremely valuable asset.

Time is for all practical purposes a non-renewable resource. As such, it becomes by all commercial standards a more highly valuable resource. I contend, therefore, that both individually and as a Christian community, we grossly undervalue time, and for that reason it is rarely seen as a true asset of worth. Oddly enough, despite our society's obsession with material wealth, even the most cursory review of philanthropic giving trends, especially as they pertain to religion, prove that time is the first and most compelling principle of good stewardship. Of time, talent, and treasure, time is the first amongst equals. Hence, despite the conventional fixation of most stewardship committees on money, I submit that time and talent deserve attention first.

Time & Talent

The traditional description of stewardship as having three major aspects, time, talent and treasure, is appropriate. Moreover, the ordering of these three aspects represents a sound basis for people to engage naturally in stewardship. The amount of money donated to charity is not the only measure of good stewardship, nor, as will be demonstrated by data from several studies, should it be the first.

Time, talent and treasure are so intrinsically intertwined that those who are willing to give one are most likely to give the others. Statistics verify what Christian churches have always held (if not taught) about the triune nature of stewardship: those who give their time and talents are most likely to give their treasure, and moreover, are most willing to do so *meaningfully* in just that order. Hence, the need to reach out to younger and newer members, especially the un-churched, converts to the Christian faith, or even those of differing confessional backgrounds, is immediate. Because stewardship is a vocational, and therefore lifelong, journey, it is often years before inward reflection upon good stewardship bears fruit in such outward signs as the generous offering of time, talent and treasure.

Asking people to give of their time (to volunteer) from the very beginning of their life in the congregation is not a matter of enticing people into a "comfort zone" whereby they are more likely to give money too, but is rather the appropriate development and outward expression of the inward change that occurs when the individual engages more deeply in the mystery of faith and the life of the congregation. Time is also the only real forum in which talents can be given and, as such, the generous offering of time is most often synonymous with the gift of talent.

Of those who contribute to charity in the United States, households with at least one family member who is actively engaged in some sort of volunteerism give, on average, twice the amount of households where no one volunteers. In 1999, volunteering households gave, on average, 2.5% of their household income to charity, while non-volunteering households donated only 1.2%.[5] In short, it is significant to note the following:

- Households which engaged in volunteerism gave substantially more than households that did not. Amongst households which gave to charity, contributions were $2,295 from volunteers, and $1,009 from non-volunteers.
- Households with people attending religious services "on a regular basis, at least once or twice a month, gave more than

---

[5] Independent Sector, "The Relationship Between Giving and Volunteering," *Giving and Volunteering in the United States, Findings from a National Survey* (Washington D.C.: Independent Sector, 1999).

twice as much annually as those who were not regular attendees."[6]

- "People who regularly attended religious services volunteered at a much higher rate (54%)" than those who did not attend religious services on a regular basis (32%).[7]
- People were "much more likely to volunteer" when asked (63%) than to step forward unasked (25%).[8]
- The average number of hours per week, per volunteer, was 3.7–3.8 hours,[9] and the estimated hourly rate of volunteer time was approximately $15.40 per hour.[10]

Despite such promising signs amongst donors and volunteers, it should be noted that in the United States, the number of people giving to religious causes continues to decline. In the late 1990s alone, Independent Sector's national survey indicated that the "percentage of total respondents giving to religion declined from

---

[6] Independent Sector, "Giving in the United States," *Giving and Volunteering in the United States, Key Findings* (Washington D.C.: Independent Sector, 2001).

[7] *Ibid.,* "Volunteering in the United States."

[8] *Ibid.*

[9] Independent Sector, "The Demographics of Household Contributors and Volunteers," *Giving and Volunteering in the United States, Findings from a National Survey* (Washington D.C.: Independent Sector, 1999).

[10] Independent Sector, "Volunteering in the United States," *Giving and Volunteering in the United States, Key Findings* (Washington D.C.: Independent Sector, 2001). Independent Sector bases the hourly value of volunteer time on the average wage of non-agricultural workers, as given each year by *The Economic Report of the President*, plus a 12% allowance for fringe benefits.

48% in 1995 to 45% in 1998."[11] According to the United States Census Bureau, this would mean some 8.1 million Americans ceased giving to religious causes.[12] If applied evenly over the estimated 353,000 religious congregations in the United States[13] (83% of which are Christian), the impact becomes an issue for real concern. If the trend stayed constant (and early census indications are that it actually grew), at least 16.2 million people ceased giving to religious charities from 1995–2001.

To be sure, if the United States has lost 16 million people who had previously supported religious charities, we may safely conclude that the churches have lost people who used to volunteer their time and talents in ministry as well. Using the statistics provided by the United States Census Bureau, it could be conservatively estimated that of the 16 million people who ceased giving to religious charity, some 6.9 million people ceased to engage in volunteer ministry. At the average rate of between 3.7–3.8 hours per week, this adds up to an alarming loss of 26 million hours of volunteer ministry each and every week between 1995 and 2001.

To keep the impact of the loss of the faithful's generosity with their time in perspective, the following chart quantifies the

---

[11] Independent Sector, "The Relationship Between Religious Involvement and Charitable Behavior," *Giving and Volunteering in the United States, Findings from a National Survey* (Washington, D.C.: Independent Sector, 1999).

[12] US Census Bureau, 2000 General Census information and 1997 Economic Industry Status Report.

[13] Independent Sector, *America's Religious Congregations: Measuring Their Contribution to Society* (Washington, D.C.: Independent Sector, 2000), p. 3.

developing trends, and signals the crisis which awaits us should they go unchecked:[14]

	1995	1998	2001
Religious Givers	99,865,244	91,884,321	88,287,035
Number of Volunteers	42,942,054	39,510,258	37,963,425
Volunteer Hours	1.61 billion	1.48 billion	1.42 billion

According to the 2001 Key Findings of the Independent Sector report, *Giving & Volunteering in the United States,* the average value attached to volunteer work is figured at a rate of $15.40 per hour. Even if the required hours were picked up by secular non-profit agencies, to pay for what was once given freely would require a shocking $21 billion a year in increased charitable giving. Since all indications are that those who are religiously observant give almost twice as much as the average American, it follows that it will take almost twice as many donors to raise this deficit in real dollar terms.

But more than this, Christians live under a dominical and moral imperative to love their neighbors. It would be immoral to expect "others" to pick up ministries which the churches have traditionally and necessarily provided. Our obligation as lovers of humanity is not financial alone: indeed money by itself is incapable

---

[14] There are several assumptions in this chart, including that trends will stay constant over the next 20 years. Further, this chart assumes that the trend toward increased giving amongst a smaller number of people will continue at current levels. The data is presented with a view to addressing the methodology, criticisms and findings of John & Sylvia Ronsvalle in their paper, "Giving to Religion: How Generous Are We?," Copyright 1998 Christian Century Foundation. Cited by permission from the June 3–10, 1998 issue of the *Christian Century.* Subscriptions: $49/yr. from P.O. Box 378, Mt. Morris, IL 61054. 1-800-208-4097.

of love. We, as Christians, more than being obliged, are truly dedicated to the welfare of humanity. Only in the hand of a lover—of one who is prepared to devote time, and talent—can money make any difference at all in the lives of people.

The possibility that attendance at worship services will either remain stagnant or decline, with the corollary loss of volunteer ministry, has the potential to be devastating to society in the near term. With both the American and Canadian governments entering into more and more public-private partnerships in order to deliver critical social services, the local church, lacking volunteers, will be decreasingly able to fill the gaps. Should this happen, not only will churches become less significant to society, thereby furthering the societal paradigm shift toward secularity, but we will leave ourselves unable to express in individual, visible, external signs the promises of our profession of faith. After all, in addition to our need to engage in worship and ministry (both of which take abundant resources), churches are entrusted with the dignity of being the face of Christ to the world. This is who we are. Hence, what is at stake is our very being.

Accordingly, churches must reinvigorate stewardship and attendance in order to meet the needs of society at large. Civics programs have all but disappeared, and with fewer people volunteering their time each and every year, the likelihood that this trend will self-correct is unrealistic. Who then will teach philanthropy—churches that believe in the cause of humanity, or secular fundraisers and consultants who operate for-profit commercial enterprises? Churches will not only serve themselves better by encouraging passionate stewardship, but in recovering stewardship from fundraising, they will preserve their ethical, moral and practical relevance to humanity.

Treasure
Churches are rightly concerned about their relevance to humanity. The future not only indicates a dwindling number of

"donors," but of worshipers as well. After all, it is highly unlikely that people who quit giving to religious causes will continue to attend worship services. Obviously, this has implications for both evangelism and the internal teaching ministry. A congregation which fails to bear witness to its first principles, whether in word or deed, runs the risk of disaffecting those who come to it expecting a community which has the fortitude and conviction to withstand the influences of transient secular values.

More to the point for our purposes, it is clear that apart from a successful evangelistic initiative, the local church will matter to an ever shrinking number of people. Besides this, the local church must cope with demographic trends which are beyond its control. Consider the premise of Canadian David Foot's book, *Boom, Bust & Echo*,[15] which maps the implications of an aging and affluent baby boom giving way to a smaller and less affluent "bust" generation. Even without a decline in the percentage of people who are religiously observant, the aging and consequent demise of a disproportionately large and wealthy segment of the general population ensures that many churches in North America will be much smaller. When this occurs many churches will find themselves devoid of the people who currently engage in volunteer ministry, and less capable of providing the large financial resources they need. With this crisis on the horizon, recovering Christian stewardship becomes even more urgent every day.

In addition to the number of people attending churches, we should also consider the faithful's current understanding of stewardship and generosity. While there has been some indication that the faithful are responding to the need for better offerings at present (the average U.S. donation to religion grew from $868 in

---

[15] David Foot, *Boom, Bust & Echo: How to Profit from the Coming Demographic Shift* (Toronto: Macfarlane, Walter & Ross, 1996).

1995 to $1,002 in 1998),[16] statistics show that the increase in giving is occurring primarily amongst older members, who are at present a disproportionately large group within many historic denominations.

This reliance upon a single constituency to provide the lion's share of the resources for the ministry of the whole congregation can be characterized as "institutional welfare," and this situation has caused a crisis of imbalance in Christian stewardship. Congregations can expect to suffer a significant blow as their senior members become increasingly frail, and ultimately die. Unless congregations act quickly to correct this imbalance by teaching good stewardship to successive generations, they will face a decline in resources of critical proportions in the next few decades. This dynamic is true for most churches, though exceptionally less amongst evangelical Christian communities and "para-church" organizations which have generally been more successful in eliciting the involvement of younger persons and usually have a more age-diverse balance within their congregations.

The imbalanced reliance upon the older generation has led some to speak of what is often described as "donor fatigue." This is far too simplistic a diagnosis. Certainly, "donor fatigue" is not a universal dynamic in religious communities, although it may well apply to the 20%—generally older members—who have always been relied upon to provide 80% of the resources. If members reach the point of complaining of "donor fatigue" it may have less to do with a sense of having been overly generous with their personal time, talents and treasure, than of carrying an undue and disproportionate burden on behalf of the whole community.

---

[16] Independent Sector, "The Relationship Between Religious Involvement and Charitable Behavior," *Giving and Volunteering in the United States, Findings from a National Survey* (Washington, D.C.: Independent Sector, 1999).

When members do raise the issue of "donor fatigue," whether they name it as such or not, their concerns need to be taken seriously. In contemplating the cause for such expressions, the congregation needs to ask itself several questions:

1. Has the congregation traditionally over-relied upon a few, or particular, households for a disproportionate financial commitment?
2. How often does the congregation ask for an extraordinary financial commitment?
3. Does the congregation have a real plan to meet its anticipated needs, or is it reactive, and therefore dependent upon crisis-based giving?
4. Does this expression of "fatigue" reflect a concern about the call upon personal time, talent and treasure, or a sense rather that the community as a whole is not being challenged to be proportionately generous?
5. Has the congregation done a good job of expressing its sincere gratitude to its stewards?

The pattern of reliance upon the affluence and generosity of its elder members will be broken either by the congregation engaging in real stewardship renewal, or the natural mortality of a significant number of the faithful over the next few decades—whichever comes first. If the congregation is to have a future, we must be proactive. We may begin by engaging those already in the pews more deeply in their personal faith journey, explicitly inviting them to participate more fully in the various ministries of the congregation. At the same time, we will need to induct newcomers into a life of passionate stewardship from the beginning of their association with the congregation, so that it becomes seamlessly integrated into their understanding and practice of their personal spiritual and religious life.

It is important to treat the issue of individual stewardship as over against major giving and financial donations by institutions. In 1998, individual Americans gave an estimated $133 billion to charity. By 2000, personal giving amongst Americans was estimated to exceed $152 billion—an increase of 4.9% over individual donations to charity in 1999. Religious charitable giving

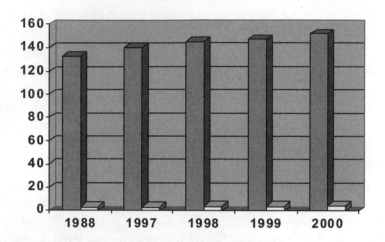

accounts for $74.3 billion or 48% of this figure.[17] However, it should be noted that the religious percentage share of overall giving is shrinking. To be more direct, even though more money is flowing to religious charities than ever before, fewer donors are responsible for these gifts, and the growth in secular charitable gifts is quickly outpacing religious giving.[18]

Individual Canadians are also generous when it comes to charity. Canadians gave in excess of $4.5 billion in 1997, and by

---

[17] Melissa S. Brown, ed., *Giving USA 2001* (Indianapolis: American Association of Fundraising Counsel [AAFRC] Trust for Philanthropy, 2001), p. 156.

[18] *Ibid.*

2000 were estimated to have given just over $5 billion[19]. While North America might be considered a largely homogeneous society, the differences in culture and charitable giving are as diverse *among* Americans and Canadians as they are *between* them. All sorts of demographic discriminators come into play: regions, language, religion, ethnic and cultural provenance, socio-economic status, and so on. The issue for Canadian givers isn't whether "it will play in Peoria" but rather "what plays in Toronto doesn't always play in the Prairies."

Conventional wisdom suggests that with the growth in secular philanthropy outpacing religious charity, religious communities need only more fully embrace secular fundraising. But as previously noted, this could not be more wrongheaded. The local church may technically be classified a "non-profit" organization, but it is much more than that. The congregation is a voluntary association of individuals who share a confession of faith, and who form communities, not organizations. While secular non-profit organizations may be willing to hire out every task that needs to be done, this is not the local church's way. The congregation is a community, not a pool of "donor prospects" who, if alienated, can be replaced by the next direct mailing or telemarketing campaign for "yet-to-be-identified donors." Secular fundraising practices affect their client membership and donors differently than they would a congregation. We thus adopt such practices at our own peril. It is time to reclaim the radical uniqueness of the Church.

If we simply jump on the bandwagon, administering "stewardship campaigns" which are little more than financial campaigns, and mimic secular models where *donations* are sought as the highest goal, the congregation has little future. By contrast,

---

[19] Adapted from: Statistics Canada, *Caring Canadians, Involved Canadians: Highlights from the National Survey of Giving, Volunteering and Participating [NSGVP],* Catalogue no. 71-542-XIE, 1997 & 2000, p. 10.

if the congregation engages in true stewardship, where *gifts* are sought, the result will not only be more financial resources for God's ministry to the world, but more members who are willing to give of their time and talent as well. The distinction between a donation and a gift is not merely semantic: a *donation* is motivated by the recognition of need; a *gift* proceeds as a faithful sharing of one's plenty out of gratitude for grace.

In abandoning the shallow and empty promises of secular fundraising, and turning to real stewardship, the congregation will help its people live out their vocations as Christians. Passionate stewardship calls us to recognize that all that we are and have is gift. It comes from God, belongs to God, and is meant for the purposes of God: it is only in our possession "in trust," as it were. We are the stewards of *God's* grace, freely and generously given for Jesus' sake. Hence we are enabled to give from the abundance of God's own blessing, and to give sacrificially. Giving in this way is so much richer a transaction than parting with a sum of money we believe to be our own in order to meet some perceived need. It is not need which churches should be promoting, but grace; not what is missing, but what *is*; and only thus will stewardship be returned to our sense of vocation as Christians, and the congregation itself to a more moral, ethical and financially steady footing.

Chapter IV
Faithfulness in a Troubled Church –
Individual Stewardship

Hope and faith are at the heart of our profession as Christians. And yet, there is much in our Christian experience which discourages us, and specifically, which threatens our cheerful contribution to the work and needs of the congregation.

In recent years, many historical denominations have been rocked by high profile and disturbing scandals, ranging from sexual exploitation by clergy or members of religious communities, for instance at Canada's Mount Cashel Orphanage and most recently in the Roman Catholic Archdiocese of Boston and elsewhere in the United States, to the Residential Schools crisis in Canada, involving the Anglican, United, Presbyterian and Roman Catholic Churches. Other denominations may have been spared public scandals because they did not participate, for example, in operating residential schools on behalf of the Canadian government. Nevertheless, it is clear that sexual abuse is present in all denominations. Attention has also been called to the more global pains and memories of Jewish communities, Armenians, and the Orthodox, to whom Pope John Paul II repeatedly apologized on behalf of the Roman Catholic Church in anticipation of the millennial year.

Through our membership in the Communion of Saints, and our participation in a living history, we all share in the responsibility for the suffering such sin has caused in the past. Likewise, we are members of a Communion where sin exists now, and we therefore live in need of continual repentance and reconciliation. The sad truth is that many of these events, past and present, have sometimes discouraged even the most devoted of Christians from generosity to the institutional church, and provided yet others convenient and ample excuse for withholding their time, talent and treasure. While at times such protest proceeds from a genuine sense of hurt and anguish, the refusal to continue as good stewards, withholding gifts of appreciation for God's bounty, frequently stems from another, ulterior, motive—namely, the desire for political or social gain.

How shall we get past our disappointment, and even disillusionment, with the institutional church? Clearly, such events have had a deleterious impact on how we fulfill our vocation as Christian stewards. Paradoxical though it may seem, however, it is no contradiction to assert that the Church as Body of Christ can be *holy* while its sons and daughters are *sinful*. Indeed, this very reality is a mystery at the core of our faith, which challenges us to come to terms with, and realize, the highest ideals and truths of Christ's message of love and salvation.

We are a Church of mercy and reconciliation: we exist *because* sin exists, and because God in his mercy chose to make sinful humanity the theater of redemption. No matter how frequent or how horrible our sins may be, we are called as followers of Christ not only to forgive, but even to seek out those who have sinned against us in order to reconcile ourselves to them, and therefore mutually to God: "There can be no aspiration to divine sonship in Jesus unless there is love for one's neighbor" (cf. Mk 12:29–31; Mt 22:37–38; Lk 10:27–28).[20] If this is true of our personal relationships, it is especially true of our relationship with the

---

[20] International Theological Commission, *Memory and Reconciliation*, 2.2.

institutional Church, which is "at the same time holy and always in need of being purified, and incessantly pursu[ing] the path of penance and renewal."[21]

This has a vital bearing on stewardship. Stewardship, in so far as it entails a generous and total self-offering of love, flows most naturally and creatively from a state of grace. It follows therefore that someone who is alienated from grace, whether by reason of his or her own sin, or sin imputed to the institutional church itself, is unable fully to exercise the perfection of grace in free and cheerful self-giving. Therefore, the vocation to stewardship, if it is to be exercised effectively, cannot be undertaken apart from our vocation to reconciliation. This is true not only of individuals, who are called to seek peace with their fellow believers and with their neighbors, but also of the institutional church, which is called to seek peace with those against whom the institution, including its mothers and fathers, have sinned. It is incumbent both upon the institutional church and its individual members to consider what role their own conduct may have played, or continues to play, in the decline of stewardship amongst the entirety of the faithful.

In this regard, the institutional church must thoroughly re-examine its relationship not only with the company of the faithful, but also with our elder brothers and sisters in faith, the Jewish people, whom we have too often offended by our conduct. Reconciliation is the responsibility of all parties to a conflict or offence, not just the offender—although the offender shares a special responsibility to seek peace. Jesus taught, "If you remember

---

[21] *Lumen Gentium* I.8 in Walter M. Abbott, S.J., ed., and Joseph Gallagher, trans. ed., *The Documents of Vatican II* (America Press, 1966), p. 24. Cf. also *Unitatis Redintegratio* II.6: "Christ summons the Church, as she goes her pilgrim way, to that continual reform of which she always has need, insofar as she is a human institution here on earth." *Ibid.,* p. 350.

that your brother or sister has something against you, leave your gift there before the altar and go; first be reconciled to your brother or sister" (Mt 5:23–24).

The institutional church must be brave enough to consider more than the advice of its insurers, accountants and lawyers when one of our pastors, leaders or volunteers harm others, and invite the moral philosopher and theologian to help guide and direct its conduct, with a constant view to reconciliation. We, as institutional church, must make bold to admit our sins and failures, and to reconcile ourselves with those whom we have hurt. For many people, especially those directly harmed by a pastor or leadership, the weight the institutional church has given in the past to *legality* has served to undermine the authenticity of its claims to be the champion of *morality*. Breaking this cycle is essential to repairing the foundation of trust upon which stewardship is built.

This being said, those to whom the governance of the institutional church has been entrusted are not alone in the need for forgiveness and repentance. Many Christians have fallen into the trap of supposing the offences of others to be greater than their own. In my experience, this is a primary foundation upon which the faithful offer "reasons" not to be generous with their time, talent, and treasure. However, holding the institutional church (through the misconduct of its representatives, notably a pastor or a highly visible leader) to a higher standard than we hold ourselves interferes with our sense of justice, mercy and forgiveness. Further, it is to allow the frailty of a mere human being—even one charged with the dignity of ministering Christ to us—to come between, and outweigh, our love for God, and God's love for us.

In the course of my work with faith communities it is not uncommon for me to hear, "I won't give to the institutional church as long as there are pedophiles or money-grabbing televangelists," or, "the institutional church won't get a penny of my money during the Residential Schools lawsuits and other scandals since it will only go to lawyers anyway." These are certainly legitimate concerns, but we must ask whether they are genuine reasons, or mere excuses, for declining to be good stewards. At the same time, the institutional church might profitably consider how it has inadvertently brought this perverse consequence upon itself, through the adoption of secular fundraising practices, particularly as epitomized in the well known "Donor Bill of Rights."[22] Withholding money is the natural byproduct of a system in which a donor's *rights* are at issue, as opposed to a steward's *gifts*.

The greater truth still is that "all have sinned, and fall short of the glory of God" (Rm 3:23), and that there is none of us who does not need to attend to the log in our own eye before pointing out the speck in our brother or sister's eye (Mt 7:2–7). If we allow sin to impede our participation in the charitable stewardship of the gifts God has given us, we shall deprive all humanity of God's will for it. For sin, as we know, is an ever present reality, disfiguring daily the indelible image of Christ we profess to have through faith. Rather than withholding our gifts, we ought to give all the more generously, in the hope that our contribution, by God's grace, might help to recover the very dignity which sin degrades.

In light of these issues it may be helpful to meditate upon the practice of offering and sacrifice in the biblical narrative. Stewardship is inherently an expression of devotion to God, from whom all blessings flow. The Bible teaches that as Israel matured in faith, sacrifice and offerings came to be used not only as a means of praising and proclaiming an Almighty Creator, but also

---

[22] "The Donor Bill of Rights" (AAFRC, 2001). The American Association of Fundraising Counsel states as Right No. 5, "To receive appropriate acknowledgment and recognition." This idea belies the teaching of Jesus, "Beware of practicing your piety before others in order to be seen by them; for then you will have no reward from your Father in heaven. So whenever you give alms, do not sound a trumpet before you, as the hypocrites do in the synagogues and in the streets, so that they may be praised by others. Truly, I tell you, they have received their reward" (Mt 6:1–2).

as sin-offerings to effect reconciliation and a restoration to purity or holiness (cf. Lv 1–6). The People of God have understood the self-giving death of Jesus to fulfill this same tradition of sacrifice. That is, Jesus offers himself as an act of supreme love (*agapé*) for the Father, and for the world, and he does so not just despite, but *in response to* the corruption of the Temple cult, and the sin which surrounded him on every side.

Jesus is the embodiment of the Passionate Steward. Through the sacrificial gift of his life, Jesus underscored the unconditional nature of stewardship and sacrifice, and in this sense, his self-offering is exemplary. It was first of all a choice, freely given, made in faith, hope, and trust—and in full and explicit awareness of the failings of the People of God. The first disciples took courage from Jesus' example, and each in turn engaged in a ministry of risk and sacrifice, which in many cases meant choosing to make their own self-sacrifice in martyrdom for the sake of the Word.

The People of God are called to be the image of Christ to the world. We do this in part through sacrificial offerings of self-giving love. If we, as members of the Body of Christ, choose to withhold our involvement or offerings until such time as the institutional church is perfect and sinless, we effectively ensure that the institutional church is ill-equipped to live up to its high calling. The net effect of our protest is that we add to the brokenness of the institutional church.

In the context of Christianity, continuing to be a good steward in the midst of conflicts of conscience is not just a matter of striving through our seemingly small sacrifices to make the institutional church better; it is a matter of fidelity to our profession of faith. As individuals, we must remember how valuable the generous devotion of our time, talent and treasure is to the world around us. As the old proverb has it, it is better to light one candle than to curse the darkness. To give up our Christian vocation as stewards, or withhold our gifts until we get our way (no matter how righteous our cause), means depriving not only the institutional church, but humanity, of our gifts of time, talent and treasure. We need to remember that we take our place amidst a company of millions, who together promote everything from outreach to the poor to care of the elderly, education of the young to advocacy for the oppressed, companionship for the lonely to solitude for the overwhelmed.

Hence it is clear that should our personal disappointment in the institutional church give us cause to cease being passionate stewards, it is not just the institutional church that will suffer, but we ourselves. We can only *pray* that our individual stewardship strengthens the Body of Christ in goodness and love, but we need only look to the schools, soup kitchens, housing programs, health care networks and other ministries we undertake to *know* that our stewardship upholds countless others. So, for example, the gifts of our time and talent have helped millions of children receive the moral, religious and faith development we ourselves have held dear. We need to recognize how many important ministries will lose our valuable support if we let our anger or disappointment with individuals in the institutional church dissuade us from being good stewards. If we quit being passionate stewards, the "Out of the Cold" program for the homeless supported by our congregation will lose financial support; food that we donate through the congregation's regular collection of non-perishable goods would not get to the tables of the poor and hungry; and finally, we will find ourselves lesser people for not being true to our profession of faith.

Our pursuit of passionate stewardship constantly engages us in the senseless acts of charity and humanity that allow us to share in Christ, and which give our life true purpose and meaning. In the end, while we are not always pleased with the institutional church, we are better off for it, for it is—even in its imperfection—the well from which Christ provides our hope and salvation.

Chapter V
Nurturing the Vocation –
Corporate Stewardship

While the vocation to good stewardship belongs first to every Christian individually, it belongs also to all Christians collectively, which is to say, to the whole company of the faithful acting as the Body of Christ. God has entrusted the institutional church with marvelous gifts—including the faithful themselves; and for our benefit, he has bestowed resources such as property, food, shelter, the gospel, and the very Bread of Life, Jesus Christ. How the institutional church manages these riches is every bit as important as the carefulness and generosity with which individual Christians manage their own time, talent, and treasure. Moreover, the institutional church has a role as exemplar and teacher, and can expect that its members will take their cue from its corporate habits and rhetoric concerning stewardship. This responsibility is lodged on the one hand with the board of elders, deacons, or whatever body has authority to make decisions about the management of ecclesial resources; and on the other, with the congregations, where the Word is proclaimed, practiced and preached.

The challenge of fulfilling this responsibility is especially daunting at present. The very same factors which have conspired to bring about a decline in church attendance—and therefore, the need to do more with less—have also shaped the attitudes of those who continue to be regularly observant within the institutional church. The faithful bring with them assumptions influenced by the strong secularization of society—including an anti-institutional bias. The institutional church is not immune to the exaltation of the individual over the community, or to the spirituality of conspicuous consumption which has taken hold of the public imagination. The succession of moral scandals within the household of faith has at times fundamentally undermined the trust of believers and unbelievers alike. The erosion of trust and confidence in the integrity and leadership of the institutional church has led many members to abandon the pews. Consequently, it is a smaller congregation that must answer the call to good stewardship. Finally, this is a smaller institutional church which sometimes feels itself to be under siege, and lamentably, sometimes from within.

The challenges facing those who remain observant in the institutional church have been forcefully defined by historical, political and geographic factors, stemming from as early as the first waves of immigration to the New World. The institutional church in the New World never enjoyed anything like the monolithic stability of the institutional churches in Europe. With the urbanization of North America, and the subsequent migration to the suburbs, the one constant in the North American experience has been change itself, and the need to adapt. If we are to promote good stewardship amongst the faithful, we shall have to examine our historic decisions, and come to terms with the impact of ancient choices on modern challenges.

The Urban Experience

The settlement of the New World and the spread of Christianity across its shores created a unique situation for the institutional church. In terms of confessional faith, North American religious practice has largely been shaped by immigrant classes and their post-reformation traditions, values, and sense of *magisterium*. There has never really been a government-sponsored church in North America, despite the desire of the Church of England to keep the Anglican Church in Canada an "established Church." Indeed, religious pluralism and the many different ethno-racial waves of immigration to North America ensured that, within the context of Christianity alone, there developed traditions and practices as numerous and autonomous as the communities from which they emerged. It is not surprising then that North America's confessional and individual sense of stewardship was powerfully shaped by these influences.

New York City and Toronto provide good examples of how mainline "establishment" churches developed different, albeit related, problems due to the way urban North America was populated. In strolling the streets of New York City—Manhattan, Queens, the Bronx, or any other borough—it is not uncommon to find Roman Catholic churches within blocks of each other. Sometimes, such churches sit nearly side by side in the same block. How did this happen? Historically, when the Roman Catholic Church began receiving the seemingly endless waves of European immigrants, it set up ethnocentric congregations, preserving the language and customs of each immigrant community. This was not an attempt at segregating ethnic communities, some of whom had been at war in Europe for centuries, but rather an attempt to ensure that newly arrived immigrants, generally uneducated and largely illiterate, had their particular needs met in adapting to their new country. Accordingly, St. Patrick's Old Cathedral, the Roman Catholic *pro*-cathedral in New York, was situated in what had been the north end of the old city of New York (at 263 Mulberry Street), and became the center of the Irish community. However, the next generation of European immigrants, the Italians, shortly thereafter made their home at the Church of the Most Precious Blood (109 Mulberry Street), only two blocks south in the same neighborhood, which had now become Little Italy. A third church, Most Holy Crucifix, actually lies between these two churches within a single block of each. This situation left three thriving Roman Catholic communities within two blocks of each other, ethnically separated, but still joined in the Roman Catholic Church.

As New York City grew and expanded into suburban upstate counties, Long Island, and New Jersey, the Roman Catholic Irish and Italians who had once dominated the streets of what had become Lower Manhattan achieved a newfound sense of middle class wealth, and so migrated to the suburbs for more space and individual home ownership. What was even twenty years ago a bustling "Little Italy" near Mott and Prince Streets in New York, is now the border of Chinatown and upscale SoHo. The neighbourhood today is as strongly shaped by consumerism as it once was by Roman Catholicism.

Suburban migration did not signal the end of Roman Catholicism in the Archdiocese of New York, but it did mean that future growth would be confined primarily to the suburbs. The communicants who once populated the pews of urban churches in Lower Manhattan have made way for a more religiously diverse urban community of Chinese Buddhists, Middle Eastern Muslims, and agnostics/atheists from former communist countries. The Roman Catholic Church, however, has chosen to keep many of its urban churches open, with the result that the urban Roman Catholic Church remains property-rich, while many of the communities themselves struggle to survive. This condition begs on the churches' purse strings daily, sometimes at the expense of mission and ministry, as well as necessitating a complicated transfer of wealth around the entire Archdiocese and its schools, in order that it might remain economically viable.

Toronto, the second largest Anglican diocese in North America, suffers similarly. The post-World War I & II immigration boom, primarily from the British Isles, South Africa and other British protectorates, ensured that Toronto would be profoundly Protestant—and, in particular, Anglican—in orientation. In a pattern which paralleled the American experience in New York, it seemed to the rapidly expanding Anglican Church as if the waves of immigrants populating and overpopulating Toronto would never stop. Beginning in the early twentieth century, the diocesan Synod began an aggressive building campaign in the outer neighborhoods of Toronto and its suburbs. In the 1950s, for example, the plan was to plant a church every mile along Bloor Street, the major east-west axis of the city. By the early 1970s, however, the meteoric expansion of the Anglican Church in urban Toronto came to an abrupt halt with the cessation of the influx of British immigrants, and the marked drop in church attendance that was indicative of the times.

Today, with the amalgamation of these suburbs into a "mega-city," urban Toronto's Anglican community, like New York's Roman Catholic, has a glut of churches in the inner city. Most of these communities are based in expensive to maintain, aging, neo-gothic structures. All are in financial need. Only a few have congregations large enough to meet these needs, let alone a critical mass of the faithful capable of ministering to the neighborhoods around them. Indeed, were it not for the income from property rentals or trusts established long ago, some of these churches could not keep their doors open, let alone thrive. It is often said that the reliance upon rental income from community groups has effected a reversal in the institutional church's God-given vocation, such that the community now "ministers" to the institutional church.

The problem of being property-rich and income-poor is not a unique state for most urban churches. All over North America we need to revisit our sense that closing or consolidating urban churches somehow represents a failure. Moreover, the evangelization—or in some cases, re-evangelization—of the urban core, while always a worthy ministry, is generally unlikely to yield enough new members to compensate for the lower proportion of even nominally Christian persons and cultures represented by current urban repopulation trends. Our cities have become more ethnically and socially diverse, and the number of neighborhoods it takes to sustain a congregation today simply makes many of our churches redundant. Unless we consolidate them, or learn how to use these properties in exciting new ways to fulfill our Christian mission, we will continue to expend resources for the sole purpose of underwriting property, while possibly undermining the institutional church which could use these resources elsewhere.

The landscape of the Old World is dotted with churches now over a thousand years in ruin which once thrived, but which, through design or tragedy, outlived their viability. We must come to grips with the idea that while some of our congregations may have fulfilled an important role in their day, the changing demographics of their neighborhoods makes them no longer necessary.

Stewardship is a two-way street. Not only does it require the faithful to give generously of their time, talent and treasure. It also requires the leadership of the institutional churches to be good stewards of the resources which have been entrusted to their care and management. Aside from liberating the financial resources of a denomination from building maintenance and upkeep on what can clearly be declared excess or under-used property, the denomination can reinvigorate itself by creating congregations where members gather in sufficient numbers to breathe joy, life and a sense of unity into the community. While the decision to close or merge congregations is always difficult, we must recommit ourselves to the premise that *the Church is not the building: it is the community of faith.* Liberating ourselves from the constraints of any particular property can free the institutional church to rededicate itself to fulfilling the Gospel message, and helping us to live out our vocations as Christians.

The Suburban and Rural Experience

For congregationalists, the issue of urban repopulation has a limited effect, since the viability of any given congregation is self-dependent. Many congregationalist, evangelical, and non-denominational community churches are "destination churches;"

that is to say, people come to them to satisfy a particular need, whether it be the preaching, a particular ministry, expression or understanding of confessional beliefs, or some other feature which fulfils their individual spirituality. But for the mainline, historic churches—and particularly those with a more centralized or episcopal governance—there is a mutual, even symbiotic, interdependence between individual communities of faith. When one part of the institutional church gets out of balance, it affects the others, sometimes disproportionately so. For suburban and rural congregations, the imbalance is often experienced in terms of access to resources that are not always financial in nature.

Primarily due to geographical considerations, suburban and rural congregations are less likely to have ongoing and meaningful personal experiences of their leadership staff, and are therefore unintentionally formed, in even the slightest ways, towards congregationalism. Such tendencies are supported by the strong sense of individualism and rugged self-reliance that have necessarily characterized rural communities in both Canada and the United States. But more than this, when many suburban and rural congregations view themselves as being at the short end of the stick in terms enjoying the pool of leadership, expertise, and financial resources at the disposal of the wider denomination, it is no surprise that they should come to believe their relationship with the denomination or conference to be essentially economic in nature, experienced primarily as a fiscal arrangement based upon transfer payments to "downtown."

This dynamic of alienation serves only to reinforce a reductionist view of stewardship as merely financial—a genteel way of speaking about money, rather than a vocation which lays claim upon the totality of our lives, and whose demands may call us to anything but gentility. Until such time as the historic, mainline churches are able to free their resources from the tradition of urban focus, overcoming geography and cost-constraints to redeploy their leadership staff to meet the needs of suburban and rural North America *as well*, the willingness and zeal of the faithful to keep transferring their allotted payments "downtown" will continue to wane.

This is not to say that the institutional church should redeploy its resources with the ulterior motive of retaining the financial contributions of suburban and rural members. Not only would this be a particularly cynical response to suburban and rural disaffection: it would also be to miss the point. What is at stake here is the institutional church's own exemplification of the fullness of Christian stewardship, and the need to take a stand in the face of nearly irresistible pressure, both within and without, to give money unwarranted pride of place. The truth is that the suburban, and sometimes rural, lifestyle teaches people that treasure is an effective and adequate substitute for time and talent.

Consider those suburban executives who commute to the city and enjoy a large staff at work. They use business consultants to meet unfulfilled needs, rely upon day-care providers to meet family obligations, independent contractors to mow the lawn, and now have the luxury of ordering groceries over the internet and having them delivered to the door. When their daily experience has formed them to believe that money can replace their time and talents, it is easy to fall into the trap of believing that it can be equally appropriate to substitute the gift of money for the offering of time and talent in their congregation. The institutional church must take great care to stop reinforcing this prejudice through its own policies and practices. It is only by developing a fuller, more inclusive understanding of stewardship in our suburban and rural communities that we can hope to redress the current imbalance in the proper interdependency and universality of our churches.

The cultivation of good stewardship must be supported by institutional policy and example, and with an evident and uniform coherence between our teaching and our practice. Indeed, the example set by denominational or conference leadership will not only be formative for congregations, but will either put teeth in our rhetoric, or give the lie to it. If we expect people to give "a good measure, pressed down, shaken together [and] running over" (Lk 6:38), they may rightly expect that the denomination as a whole will make the very best of the gifts entrusted to it.

Chapter VI
The Faith Community –
Congregational Stewardship

If the cultivation of good stewardship begins with denominational leadership, it is most readily lived out in the context of congregational life. This is where people gather; this is where fears and concerns about the future of the Church are voiced and addressed; this is where the Word is preached; and this is where the heart and hands of Christ are opened to the world.

Church Attendance

Perhaps more than any other factor, it is the decline in local church attendance, noticeable first in mainline churches, which has created a sense of urgency with respect to matters of stewardship. The needs of God's world are as compelling as ever; the institutional church's mission is as ambitious as ever; but there are fewer people who are committed to carrying it out. When Christian communities find themselves stretched even to maintain their material infrastructure, it is small wonder that the faithful remnant is buffeted between hopelessness and hand-wringing. What, we fret, is to become of us?

But this is an unnecessarily short-sighted view of the matter. One of the Church's greatest gifts is longevity: because all time belongs to Christ, the Christian is able to take a longer view of things. The past allows us to assess our present; the future allows us to journey forward in hope. It is thus salutary to re-examine our anxiety about the current drop in church attendance. After all, the first decline in the church occurred when Peter, the rock upon whom Christ would build His Church, and all of the other apostles (except John and the women who were devoted to Christ's ministry) ran from the Cross where he hung dying. But even after denying their Savior, they returned to profess the Truth. It is humanity's sad pattern that our adherence to the institutional church waxes and wanes in tandem with our humility or devotion, our sense of shame or self-reliance.

Obviously this realization does not give us license for complacency. Our mission is bigger than we are, and it behooves us to ensure that there are stewards enough to carry it out. At the same time, we do not help ourselves by lapsing into despair. God has given his promise that not even the gates of hell shall prevail against us (Mt 16:18). Even when we fail in faithfulness, even when it looks as if the tiniest remnant is all that will be left to us, the local church continues to be an effective sign of hope and salvation.

Attendance at worship services and involvement in the institutional church has risen and fallen from the beginning. Almost every century has seen the Body of Christ both triumphant and humbled, often within only a few short years of each other. When the bubonic plague ravaged Europe and the masses saw their pastors and leaders dying the same horrible deaths as the vilest of sinners, many people abandoned the Church. Only decades later, the Renaissance marked a new age of religious zeal and promise for the Church. This ebb and tide of church attendance has characterized Christianity throughout history.

It is helpful to remember that in our lifetime, especially during the 1960s and 1970s when church attendance was dropping drastically in North America, it was rising exponentially in countries around the globe. In Africa the number of believers grew through evangelization, while in Poland and China it remained steadfast in the face of oppression. We must recover our sense of ourselves as Christians, individually as a consequence of our profession of faith and baptism, but corporately linked to one another in the worldwide struggle for salvation. If we fail to do this we are bound to see only that which is before our eyes daily—to take the short view—and our lives will be terribly limited. How depressing it would be for us if our values were powerless to transcend our experiences.

Hospitality and Reception

Within congregations, our anxiety about church attendance sometimes spills over into the way we view seekers and newcomers. The tendency is to see the newcomer as a potential donor, or a committee member—as someone who will help us to carry the burden of ministry. But this is essentially to objectify people, valuing them for what they may be able to give, rather than for who they are. The newcomer is himself or herself a gift whom God has offered to the congregation. How we receive, care for, study, learn from, develop, interact with, and deploy that gift is a matter of stewardship.

How we receive inquirers and newcomers when they cross the threshold impacts greatly on how they perceive our community. Taking the time to teach volunteers how properly to exercise a ministry of hospitality towards seekers is probably one of the most rewarding aspects of our vocation as stewards. It is not enough simply to smile and hand newcomers a leaflet, bulletin or an order of service; we must genuinely greet and accept them. In this regard, there is no better model for Christian hospitality and welcoming than Mary, who chose to receive the Christ-child in her womb without knowing exactly what it would entail for her life, or the path of salvation for humanity. Mary's hospitable reception of the Christ-child in response to God's plan for humanity was a choice, not an obligation. She made room for Him freely, offering herself, her time, her innate gifts for motherhood, and the totality of her meager resources, for the sake of a nascent Promise.

We are called to devote our time, talent and treasure to the whole life of the Body of Christ, not just church buildings and administration. This includes first of all, people. Revisiting how we individually and institutionally receive seekers and visitors reveals a great deal about our commitment to individual Christian development and evangelization. Devoting our time and talent to the Christian tradition of hospitality, ensuring that our guests receive our very best care, and meeting their individual needs does not compete with our institutional needs. It is a crucial aspect of real evangelization.

We cannot expect, or have as an ulterior motive for welcoming guests, increasing attendance. Rendering the gift of our time, the first of the triune aspects of stewardship, in the personal, religious and educational development of those who choose to enter our congregations is essential to individual and communal evangelization. To this end, establishing stewardship education as a vocational priority for those who come to share our congregational life will do much to reverse the reduction of stewardship to the exchange of money. Time is valuable. How we choose to spend it, and equally, *when* we choose to spend it is important. Nothing puts a newcomer off faster than being mobbed in short order by the Volunteer Recruitment Committee, the Finance Committee Chair, or the congregational administrator, before being shown true hospitality.

Education

The crisis of our diminished understanding of Christian stewardship must also receive its due attention in Christian education and development. Few church or Sunday school programs take stewardship education seriously for our young. Maybe because stewardship has been reduced over the years to the idea of a financial transaction, something that many people find uncomfortable discussing, the subject is left almost exclusively to parents. By limiting stewardship to money we have made it a topic too private to discuss. We must not only recover our understanding of Christian stewardship, but develop a healthier attitude about the issue of money itself.

In the gospels, Jesus speaks often and freely about money—indeed, seemingly more than about any other subject. When you add to this his teachings about the gifts of talent and time, the Gospel can be seen to convey a strong imperative to vocational stewardship. We must learn to talk about stewardship in this vocational sense, as Christ did, even if it means learning to speak about money and resources in new and healthier ways. If we do not begin to educate our youth, or to include instruction on stewardship in the reception of adults through renewal programs, we should not be surprised that stewardship is perceived as an unimportant aspect of the examined Christian life.

Community Life

Embracing our lives as stewards must also find expression in the ways by which we organize our congregational life. While Roman Catholic Canon Law encourages the faithful to work in consultation with their pastor on issues of financial management and stewardship, other faith traditions have gone further and entrusted the issue of stewardship primarily to the members. Either way, stewardship is the vocation of every Christian, and the more a congregation can involve the members in related decision-making, the more stewardship will be "owned" as a communal and individual pursuit. There is profound truth in Jesus' observation, "Where your treasure is, there your heart will be also" (Mt 6:21). If individuals are encouraged to use their talents and time (which is increasingly valued in our fast-paced world) in community governance, ministry and activities, then they will take the life of the community to heart.

A stewardship committee should be an important part of the life of every congregation. Such a committee can strongly influence members to volunteer their time for the Church's ministries, to offer their talents in the life of the congregation—whether as an artist, teacher, baker, bookkeeper or anything in between—and to encourage generosity of financial resources as well. Congregations that promote a balanced approach to stewardship discover what statistics prove, namely that those who volunteer their time and talents are most likely to be equally generous with their money. One leads to the other: the result is that good stewardship makes a good steward better.

The cultivation of good stewardship is most readily undertaken at the congregational level, and it reaches into every aspect of congregational life, because people, and the gifts God has given us for ministry, populate every aspect of congregational life. This is why it matters so much how we treat, or "steward" each other, how respectful we are of each other's time or person, how open we are to each other's gifts, or how grateful and accountable for each other's money. We need to teach good stewardship, to be sure; but what we say will be neither more nor less important than what we do.

Chapter VII
Why Give? A Comparison of Secular and Christian Motivations for Philanthropy

Experience shows that the inability of pastors and volunteer ministers to identify and articulate the values which promote good stewardship is a primary source of the confusion between secular fundraising practices and Christian stewardship principles. The commercial culture in which fundraising has thrived and prospered often runs counter to the nature, teaching and leading of stewardship as a *ministry* within the congregation. Unfortunately, the way in which "stewardship" has been practiced over the centuries has led to its devaluation as a ministry, especially amongst pastors, who often see stewardship programs and financial campaigns as competing with their ability to provide pastoral care, worship and other ministries.

Until such time as both pastors and members value stewardship as a ministry, it will remain relegated to an inconvenient "necessity." Yet stewardship is one means by which we may demonstrate our faith in action. The local church is "frequently in a position to talk with people about the values and ideals of their faith."[23] In this more excellent approach to stewardship the

---

[23] Thomas H. Jeavons and Rebekah Burch Basinger, *Growing Givers' Hearts: Treating Fundraising as Ministry* (San Francisco: Jossey-Bass, 2000), p. 18. This material is used by permission of John Wiley & Sons, Inc.

congregation can recover its moral character through practice. This idea of demonstrating our faith by our actions was embodied in the admonition of St. Francis of Assisi, "Preach the gospel always; and when necessary, use words."

It serves us well, therefore, to state as clearly as possible some of the fundamental differences both in the money-raising process, and in the very motivation and premises upon which fundraising and stewardship plans are *generally* based.

Different Approaches to Giving
Christian Stewardship versus Secular Fundraising

Christian Stewardship	Secular Fundraising
Primarily concerned with the development of individuals and their place as members of the Body of Christ	Primarily concerned with the organization meeting its financial obligations
Seeks life-long change for individual	Seeks to reach an immediate financial goal
Concerned with the vocational development of the individual	Concerned with the financial commitment of the individual
Based on respect for individuals and their place in community of faith	Based on estimation of the wealth of individuals and their social standing
Promotes altruistic acts of compassion	Promotes recognition for acts of contribution

Invites everyone to be generous according to their ability	Invites a select number of wealthy individuals to make pace-setting gifts
Creates a plan based upon core beliefs and confession of faith	Creates a marketing plan to persuade or manipulate people into giving money
A vocation to goodness emanating from a confession of faith and immersion in two millennia of Christian history, culminating in a baptismal covenant with God	A process of practices and conduct predicated upon a legalistic approach focused on the individual, culminating in a "donor bill of rights" governed by an association of "professionals"
Provides an opportunity for people to give witness to their faith in proportional means	Provides an opportunity for people to self-identify their level of commitment, e.g. "Sustaining Member"
Concerned with retaining each and every member of the faith community	Concerned about growing the database, even at the expense of some current donors
Believes that offerings stem from people's commitment to their faith and community	Believes that donations are the best way to build commitment from the database of donors
Thematically promotes the idea that giving is a sign of appreciation and returns to God that which is God's own creation	Thematically promotes the idea that people are the masters and possessors of their own wealth, and that a gift can promote their standing

Approaches individuals with the hope and promise of promoting stewardship, religious values and spiritual growth	Objectifies individuals, treating them as problems to be "solved" in order to meet financial goals and organizational objectives

The foregoing chart is by no means a complete contrast between good stewardship practices, values and motivation, and secular fundraising. It is, however, an evaluative tool by which an individual and/or a faith community might begin to identify those premises which have shaped their own practices. It is especially important to examine the theological suitability of the assumptions upon which our practices are based.

St. Thomas Aquinas' treatment of Charity in the *Summa Theologica* can be instructive in exploring our practice and understanding of stewardship. In his reply to the question, "Whether Charity is a Special Virtue, Objection 1," Thomas instructs us according to Aristotle's Ethic, "Charity is included in the definition of every virtue, not as being essentially every virtue, but because every virtue depends on it in a way..."[24] This has, in addition to scriptural teachings, shaped the Christian ethos of charity and generosity taught by the Roman Catholic Church.

The Roman Catholics are not alone, however, in the correlation of charity and stewardship. Although reprinted here in extract form, I would commend all of Article 21 of the Mennonite Confession of Faith as one of the most erudite, poetic, and faith-filled declarations concerning stewardship in the Christian corpus:

---

[24] Thomas Aquinas, *The Summa Theologica,* trans. Fathers of the English Dominican Province (New York: Benziger Bros., 1947), II-II, 23, 4 – Reply to Objection 1.

As servants of God, our primary vocation is to be stewards in God's household. God, who in Christ has given us new life, has also given us spiritual gifts to use for the Church's nurture and mission... We believe that time also belongs to God and that we are to use with care the time of which we are stewards... We acknowledge that God as Creator is owner of all things... The first church in Jerusalem put Jubilee into practice by preaching the gospel, healing the sick and sharing possessions. Other early churches shared financially with those in need. As stewards of God's earth, we are called to care for the earth and to bring rest and renewal to the land and everything that lives on it. As stewards of money and possessions, we are to live simply, practice mutual aid within the church, uphold economic justice and give generously and cheerfully... We are called to be stewards in the household of God, set apart for the service of God...[25]

It seems that despite the "scandal of division" which has fractured the Body of Christ these many centuries, the Christian understanding of stewardship remains a cohesive and theologically shared value, even if practiced differently according to confessional tradition. Such widespread agreement is testament to the truth of this core understanding, and to the teachings of Christ Jesus. Hence, the longer we allow our stewardship practices to give counter-witness to our faith, abetted by the divisiveness inherent in the secular practice of "targeting," "segmenting" and "prospecting" members, the more difficult it will be for the institutional church to thrive, inter-confessionally, or universally. For this reason, stewardship need not be approached from a confessional perspective, but from its collectively embraced center,

---

[25] "Article 21: Christian Stewardship," *Confessions of Faith in a Mennonite Perspective* (Scottdale: Mennonite Publishing House, 1995).

based in Scripture, the Body of Christ, and our continual pursuit of unity.

This said, aside from the deleterious impact that *secular* fundraising has had upon the institutional church, the implementation of some of our *own* ancient practices can also be an impediment to good stewardship. Despite the intense criticism it will invite, I believe we must revisit our understanding of the tithe, and its place in the institutional church today.

The tithe, as described in the Pentateuch, became the predicate definition of all non-holocaust and animal sacrifice in Israel. Consider these citations from sacred Scripture:

> Jacob made a vow saying, "If God will be with me, and will keep me in this way that I go, and will give me bread to eat and clothing to wear, so that I come again to my father's house in peace, then the Lord shall be my God, and this stone which I have set up for a pillar, shall be God's house; and of all that you give me I will surely give one tenth to you" (Gn 28:20–22).

> All tithes of herd and flock, every tenth one that passes under the shepherd's staff, shall be holy to the Lord. Let no one inquire whether it is good or bad, or make substitution for it... These are the commandments that the Lord gave to Moses for the people of Israel on Mount Sinai (Lv 27:32–34).

In each of these instances a legalistic approach to stewardship was developed. The quantification of stewardship became a measure not only of 10% of a Jewish household's income and possessions, but the "first fruits," i.e. the best of a household's income and possessions. As the tithe became embraced as part of the Mosaic "Law," it further became incumbent upon Jewish households to fulfill the letter of the law, the "full tithes."

> Bring the full tithe into the storehouse, so that there may be food in my house, and ... then see if I will not open the windows of

heaven for you and pour out for you an overflowing blessing (Mal 3:10).

Generosity and giving in Israel, however, were not limited to the tithe. For the most part, the offerings of Jews could be categorized in three major ways: sacrifices to God, which were primarily holocaust sacrifices; tithing to the religious community, which would evolve into the support of the Temple cult and local synagogues; and extraordinary offerings (sometimes referred to as free will offerings), to celebrate or memorialize special occasions, both joyous and sad. It should be noted that the tithe was not a "guilt" or "sin" offering, but rather an ongoing gift to God of one's abundance in return for the bounty that was bestowed upon the individual (life, joy, property, wealth, etc.).

As for the extraordinary offerings, while they sometimes were associated with sin or guilt, as were holocaust offerings, they were distinctive in that they were made over and above the regular offerings (tithes), either for joyous thanksgiving to God at such times as birth, presentation at the Temple, victory in war; or equally at times of sorrow, to commemorate a loss, such as death or defeat. They were distinguished from regular (tithe) offerings, however, in that they were not legally prescribed by the law, obligation, guilt or sin.

Since the destruction of the second Temple during the sacking of Jerusalem in 70 C.E., there have been no animal or holocaust sacrifices amongst either the Jewish people, or the sect that would become the Christian Church. However, the theme of "obligatory offerings," the tithe, and extraordinary giving, remain part of the Judeo-Christian tradition to this day. For this reason it is important to examine how these two forms of giving survive in contemporary theology and practice.

The Tithe

Many Christian traditions and communities teach their members and adherents to be the faithful to tithe. Without undermining the promotion of generosity, we need to revisit the theological basis by which they do so. In particular, it is important to review the context in which tithing was practiced and promoted in the "Law" of Israel.

The tithe, though clearly required by God in the Torah, was part of a complicated and comprehensive legalistic approach to Jewish life, worship, and the demonstrative provision of monetary support to Jewish society. What is often lost on those who advocate tithing is the larger context in which it was inextricably taught and practised. While "the Law" required that a Jewish household provide 10% of its finest wealth and possessions in support of the Jewish people and in thanksgiving, it also stipulated an equally specific system of related financial practices. The Law provided a "social safety net" for the poor, providing, amongst other things, that the poor be allowed to glean from the fields to feed themselves. There were also practical ordinances like Jubilee whereby, at the change of every generation, debts were forgiven, lands were returned, and the distribution of wealth was totally restructured (though there are arguments about whether Jubilee was actually enacted).

Contemporary tithing is taught on the basis of a similarly legalistic and authoritarian approach: tithing is laid upon us as an obligation. Christ, by contrast, proclaimed a better and more compassionate reading of the Law. One thinks, for example of his elevation of marriage over the more transactional interpretation of the Mosaic Law (Mt 19:6–8). Jesus makes clear that he did not come to abolish the law but to fulfill it (Mt 5:17). By extension, we may assume that he calls us to an even higher standard than the tithe—the standard of love. It is for this reason I believe that tithing, as a teaching and practical "tool," undermines our Christian espousal of generosity by relying too heavily upon obligation, rather than joy and free will, which are at the heart of Jesus' own example of sacrifice and subjugation to the will of God.

Extraordinary Offerings

Scripture provides many examples of extraordinary offerings, given over and above the requirements of the Mosaic Law. These include, amongst others, offerings to seal a covenant (2 Sm 15:7–9) and at the termination of a covenant, such as in the story of the Nazirite (Nm 6:1–21); peace and reconciliation offerings; and offerings at the dedication of sanctuaries (1 Kgs 8:1–13) and the consecration of priests (Lv 8:1–29 and Nm 8:5–22). The practice of extraordinary offerings has continued in Christianity, but needs to be vigorously promoted as part of our ongoing stewardship, rather than being treated as an unusual practice confined to the administration of special campaigns. The restoration of extraordinary offerings as an ordinary feature of the institutional church's life is part of our journey to recover good stewardship, and entails returning such offerings to their proper place during times of joy (births, confirmation, weddings, ordinations, etc.) and times of sorrow (death, disaster, and other forms of loss).

Recovering Generosity as a Christian Value

By the time of Jesus, the disdain for the Sadducees' and Pharisees' strictly legalistic interpretation of Torah and the developing themes that would take hold in Midrash and Talmudic writings gave rise to a broader and more thematic approach to God's gift of stewardship and generosity. Indeed, at the birth of Jesus, Joseph, a poor man, made the offering of a poor man—a pair of doves or two young pigeons—in celebration and thanksgiving for the birth of his 'son,' the Messiah.[26]

---

[26] Lk 2:23–24: "…(as it is written in the law of the Lord, 'Every firstborn male shall be designated as holy to the Lord'), and they offered a sacrifice according to what is stated in the law of the Lord: 'a pair of turtledoves

The attempt to impose tithing, without implementing the totality of the socio-economic aspects of the Mosaic Law, may lead to perverse consequences, especially amongst the poor for whom 10% may represent a disproportionate burden, and even bring harm. Equally, the tithe can be contrary to the intent of the Law for people of unparalleled wealth. (If computer magnate Bill Gates were to give 10% of his vast billions, he would still live in extreme opulence and could therefore not be considered generous).[27] In promoting "percentage based giving" (such as tithing) over generosity, the Church repeats the same mistakes upon which "gift chart" based giving falters (cf. Chapter X, "The Gift Chart – Substituting Process for Values").

---

or two young pigeons.'"

[27] In the 2001 U.S. Presidential campaign Al Gore and his family were criticized for only giving $15,197 to charity in 1998, while George Bush and his family gave a whopping $334,000. However, the Gore family contributed 7% of their household income to charity while the Bushes gave 2%, setting off a heated debate about generosity within the philanthropic sector. Source: "Sharing the Wealth: Prosperous Giving in Charitable Times – Facts and Figures." Copyright 2002, Minnesota Public Radio. Reproduced with permission of Minnesota Public Radio and MPR News.

Chapter VIII
On the Law and Generosity

Tax Law

One of the greatest failings of the secular charitable sector today—and which unfortunately has been woven into the fabric of fundraising in the institutional church—is its misunderstanding of the motivation for giving. For the Christian, giving is a matter of generosity, and its motivation lies in the deepest convictions of our faith, informed by love and gratitude for grace. Secular fundraisers, however, undercut this principle when they promote tax deductions and credits as a compelling incentive for charitable giving. More than this, and ironically, statistics show that the aggressive emphasis on tax incentives as a strategy for eliciting charitable gifts, even in the secular arena, is misplaced.

In the past, social scientists, demographers and statisticians have argued that a tax code which rewards and promotes charitable giving is the reason for America's leadership in philanthropic giving. While there are significant differences in the Internal Revenue Services' Tax Code in the United States and Canada's Income Tax Act, the Canadian Income Tax Act (as amended) also vigorously promotes charitable giving, even if not at the level of the United States. However, contrary to conventional wisdom, neither has a controlling effect on how generosity is played out in the giving patterns of Americans and Canadians.

Indeed, according to Tom Cullinan, the successor of Robert Sharpe (founder of the College of William & Mary's National

Planned Giving Institute), and himself a highly regarded national leader in the area of planned giving, always reminds students about the importance of philanthropic intent. "People have been generous," says Cullinan, "with current gifts of income and estate gifts of assets, long before there were charitable tax deductions and credits. For decades, American charitable giving has maintained a fairly steady rate at 2% of the gross domestic product, despite an array of economic and other difficulties. The main exceptions (the Great Depression, World War II, and the soaring inflationary period of the 1970s) saw a shift away from current giving towards estate gifts."[28]

Some leaders in the area of philanthropy, such as Susan Tressler, who made her name in the environmental lobby, have appropriately explored the issue of tax incentives, and concluded that the belief that they are the primary reason for philanthropic generosity in the United States is largely unwarranted:

> Since passage of the U.S. Revenue Act of 1917, which stipulated tax benefits for charitable giving for the first time, philanthropy has evolved and grown in a way unmatched anywhere else in the world... In its 1993 survey, Independent Sector also explored the relationship between charitable giving and tax incentives. The findings showed that 73% of the charitable givers surveyed did not intend to use their gifts as tax deductions, suggesting other factors were influencing their decision to give.[29]

---

[28] Tom Cullinan, Lecture given at the College of William and Mary's National Planned Giving Institute, Williamsburg Va, June 2001.

[29] Susan Tressler, "Charitable Giving in the United States: A Model and Opportunity for Funding Conservation of Biodiversity" (IUCN: paper presented at the Financing Biodiversity Conference, Harare, Zimbabwe, September 1995), p.2.

To be certain, the United States Revenue Act of 1917, the Estate Tax Law of 1921, and the Gift Tax Act of 1932 have all played an integral part in the promotion of charitable giving in the United States. The tax code in the United States is now so voluminous that accountants and lawyers base entire careers on a single section of it. However, while tax policy can promote and reward charitable giving, it can never provide the basic motivation for giving.

The very definition of gift entails the free transfer of something of value, and for that reason the heart of every charitable gift must be the philanthropic intent of the giver. The assertion that tax policy is a reason for giving negates the ancient Greek notion of philanthropy as the "love of humanity" and reduces giving to a transaction, whereby the giver receives something in exchange for his or her gift. To be sure, tax credits and deductions are society's way of encouraging desirable behaviour. But even tax policy experts are adamant that tax incentives for charitable giving are not a *motivation* for giving—they are a *reward*. For this reason, in almost every jurisdiction in the United States and Canada, donors are prohibited by law from receiving something of real value in exchange for their charitable gifts, aside from those tax deductions and credits which may be available by statute or the ruling of tax administrators and the courts. The receipt of something of value mitigates the value of the gift and therefore negates its charitable status. This idea is recognized in almost every jurisdiction, and uniformly adopted as a principle of simple tax law.[30]

---

[30] Both Canada and the United States put limits on what charities can give to donors in "appreciation" for charitable gifts, though I would argue that some gifts tied to naming opportunities ought to be discouraged by tax policy, since for many industrial and business leaders the naming of a building or program plays a part in corporate marketing strategies. Mixing marketing with charitable giving should not be subsidized or encouraged.

Charles Dickens' allegorical tale of Ebenezer Scrooge exemplifies the idea that charity is dependent upon the love of humanity. It was not until the three spirits had engaged Scrooge in his own humanity, and the human condition in general, that he became charitable and generous. Tax incentives were simply not a factor in Scrooge's decision making—Dickensian England had no tax act to reward philanthropy. In the end, Scrooge chose the joy that emanated from his own acts of generosity as his only reward. This should not surprise us for, as we shall see, such choice is at the heart of the scriptural tradition of charity and generosity.

The issue then is why secular fundraising programs spend so much time treating the impact of tax incentives on the promotion of charitable gifts. As John Watts, a noted member of the faculty of the National Planned Giving Institute, points out so clearly, "generosity is an exchange of values, though the value to the donor is completing their charitable intent, not receiving 'premiums' or other forms of expensive recognition."[31] Tax treatment may be a wise consideration in how we fulfill our pledges or financial commitments, but the commitment itself flows from the desire to make a gift in the first place.

God's Law

Whatever appeal or benefits tax law may hold for prospective donors, the Christian is called to a higher standard and motivation, which is to fulfill the Law of God. The institutional church knows this. Jesus taught that the fulfillment of "the Law" lies in worship and charity—the love of God, and the love of neighbor:

> 'Love the Lord your God with all your heart, and with all your soul, and with all your mind, and with all your strength.' The

---

[31] John Watts, Lecture given at the College of William and Mary's National Planned Giving Institute, Williamsburg Va, June 2001.

second [commandment] is this, 'You shall love your neighbor as yourself.' There is no other commandment greater than these (Mk 12:30–31).

We give, and choose to give even at a cost to ourselves (which is to say, sacrificially), not to receive a reward, but because it is the right and loving thing to do.

Although we may rightly locate the obligation to good stewardship in the Law of God, it is important to note that the biblical treatment of stewardship is by no means limited to juridical or legalistic imperatives to bring offerings, nor even to stories which deal so directly with the use of one's time, talent and treasure as to be obviously on point. Scripture is rich and varied in its presentation of philanthropy. Critical to the teaching of such stories is the idea of choice. Take, for example, the story of the Good Samaritan:

> Just then a lawyer stood up to test Jesus. "Teacher," he said, "what must I do to inherit eternal life?" He said to him, "What is written in the Law? What do you read there?" He answered: "You shall love the Lord your God with all your heart, and with all your soul, and with all your strength, and with all your mind; and your neighbor as yourself." And he said to him, "You have given the right answer; do this and you will live." But wanting to justify himself, he asked Jesus, "And who is my neighbor?" Jesus replied, "A man was going down from Jerusalem to Jericho, and fell into the hands of robbers, who stripped him, beat him, and went away, leaving him half dead. Now by chance a priest was going down that road; and when he saw him, he passed by on the other side. So likewise a Levite, when he came to the place and saw him, passed by on the other side. But a Samaritan while traveling came near him; and when he saw him, he was moved with pity. He went to him and bandaged his wounds, having poured oil and wine on them. Then he put him on his own animal, brought him to an inn, and took care of him. The next day he took out two denarii, gave them to the

innkeeper, and said, 'Take care of him; and when I come back, I will repay you for whatever more you spend.' Which of these three, do you think, was a neighbor to the man who fell into the hands of the robbers?" He said, "The one who showed him mercy." Jesus said to him, "Go and do likewise" (Lk 10:25–37).

The story of the Good Samaritan is not about embracing a juridical imperative to generosity as laid down in "the Law"—let alone to receive something in return—but is rather the tale of an individual who *chose, and kept choosing,* to be a good steward despite burden and risk to himself. When a member of the priestly tribe of Israel, a Levite, chose to pass by the injured man—actually to cross to the other side of the road to avoid him—he made a choice to avoid fulfilling the intent of God's law. However, despite belonging to a despised class of un-orthodox believers, the Samaritan risked ritual uncleanness, scorn, and shunning when he chose to help the injured man. He did so first by giving of his time and talent, bandaging the man's wounds and providing the medical care of the day. Then, choosing to set aside whatever plans he surely had, he invested even more time and spent the whole night caring for a complete stranger. The next day, the Samaritan showed yet more generosity, opening his treasure to ensure that the injured man would continue to have care until he was well, promising even to ransom him from any debts he might incur during his recuperation. In thus choosing to help, the man we remember as the "Good Samaritan" engaged in the fullness of stewardship: he gave of his time, his talent, and his treasure in the aid of another, and in so doing, according to the "expert," actually fulfilled "the Law."

Stewardship is therefore analogous to the ancient Greek concept of philanthropy. For the Greeks, philanthropy was not restricted to charitable giving but was a virtuous goal which guided people's lives and to which the virtuous person aspired. In this sense, the classical Greek concept of philanthropy, as espoused by the philosopher Aristotle, shows that when it comes to the love of humanity, a reasoning society can end up sharing the same values as a religious community. Without knowing it, Aristotle pointed in his day to the fulfilment of philanthropy in the birth, death and resurrection of Jesus just as surely as the Hebrew Scriptures and wisdom literature did. After all, at base, the love of humanity is the *a priori* motivation for Christ's love act of salvation, and his ultimate sacrifice. Philanthropy in its literal and proper sense is the "love of humanity," and as such it is at the very heart of each well formed human soul, and therefore the Body of Christ.

It follows then that as people called to the imitation of Christ, the more perfectly we embrace the loving intent of the stewardship Jesus described in the parable of the Good Samaritan, the more Christ-like we become. The truth is, the more we enmesh ourselves in the human condition the more likely we are to be charitable. There is no better place to do this than the institutional church, which encourages us to embrace our individual humanity and to place it at the service of all. For this reason, the institutional church needs to place the promotion of tax credits in its proper context. It needs to be understood as a blessing which permits the believers to leverage the love gift they had already decided in their own heart to share out of their own resources. We cannot allow "professional fundraising experts" to co-opt our message of love and compassion—stewardship—into a simple business transaction for the purposes of preserving wealth (which is, after all, at the heart of all tax planning).

Our love of neighbor is a powerful call upon our time, talent, and treasure. The teachings and history of the institutional church give us the strength and wisdom to engage fully in humanity, and therefore, to be generous stewards; for we are called to a higher standard, a higher law—the law of love. This is our faith promise confirmed by baptism!

Chapter IX
Historic Methods that have Undermined the Church's Values

One of the ploys that has been promoted by secular fundraisers, and which has frequently crept uncriticized into institutional church campaigns is the "donor recognition program." Secular fundraisers, having noted a tendency amongst contemporary donors to ask, "What's in it for me?," have been quick to rustle up a response and provide donors anything from dinner with the principal ballerina, to a name plaque on the hospital wall.

This, however, is not the Christian way. In their 1993 pastoral letter, *Stewardship: A Disciple's Response*, the National Conference of Catholic Bishops took a "comprehensive view of stewardship, describing it as a '… sharing, generous, accountable way of life.'"[32] Nowhere in this characterization of stewardship is there a mention of reward or recognition. Stewardship is the generous spending of ourselves in the fulfillment of our profession of faith, and could accurately be described as all that we do after we say, "I will, with God's help." In this understanding of stewardship, gifts are freely and happily given; they are generous and accountable, a visible sign of worship and gratitude to God.

---

[32] USCCB, "Stewardship: A Disciple's Response" (Washington, D.C.: USCCB Publishing, 1993), p. 5.

The institutional church, although it is not alone in this, has so thoroughly relied upon the skill and teaching of secular fundraisers that we have all but forgotten the wisdom of our own tradition, and seem unable to distinguish between good theology and secular grabs for money. This situation is exacerbated by the fact that secular fundraisers, in the attempt to speak the language of their church clients, have created an *apologia pecuniae seculariae* (a secular fundraising apologetic) in order to justify their methods in the context of faith communities.

Many Christians within the Roman Catholic tradition, for example, are familiar with the so-called "quadrilateral" approach to authority, whereby believers appeal to the nexus of Scripture, tradition, reason, and experience in assessing the admissibility of a proposed view or action. Some secular fundraisers have coopted the language of the quadrilateral ideal, but have distorted it by over-emphasizing experience and the place of reason. The results are more in keeping with the teachings of an MBA program than the theology of the Christian faith.

So for example, a secular fundraising apologetic would justify donor recognition programs on the grounds that *experience* shows they elicit larger gifts—and since the object of the campaign is to raise money, the practice must therefore appeal, *ipso facto*, to *reason*. Donor recognition has become such a staple of secular fundraising that hardly anyone questions it. Indeed, secular fundraisers often cite the practice of some mainline Protestant churches of naming churches for their benefactors as an example of the appropriateness of such donor recognition programs as "naming opportunities." Seldom does one hear an objection that all we have comes from the hand of God: it was never our own to offer in the first place, let alone for which to receive credit or reward.

Donor recognition presents three fundamental problems for Christians. First, for the passionate steward, donor recognition has less to do with an expression of gratitude than an appeal to vanity.

One who gives for the sake of having his or her name publicly displayed is motivated more by the esteem of peers than obedience to the call of the Holy Spirit to share, or even divest oneself of, what wealth one has.

Secondly, because donor recognition is inevitably tied to the size of a gift, rather than the generosity with which it is given, the sacrificial offerings of the un-moneyed are automatically devalued and discounted. Where are the plaques on church walls commemorating the women who worked their fingers to the bone cleaning the church, polishing brass, or appearing at the drop of a hat to cater funeral receptions? What about the laborer who gave up his vacation to help pay for a new youth worker? Or the woman on welfare who pledged a dollar a week to the building campaign? And meanwhile, a $10,000 gift from an individual who recently gave $20,000 to the Symphony, and whose disposable income sits comfortably in six figures, is memorialized with fanfare and wall plaques.

In short, congregations must not promote a system by which recognition is arbitrarily showered upon the wealthy, but rather should set a standard as radical as the Gospel itself. Our gratitude and admiration belong to generosity, not wealth. And generosity is within the reach of the poorest of the poor. Jesus' story of the widow's mite is the *locus classicus* for the call to generosity:

> [Jesus] sat down opposite the treasury and watched the people putting money into the treasury, and many of the rich put in a great deal. A poor widow came and put in two small coins, the equivalent of a penny. Then he called his disciples and said to them, "In truth I tell you, this poor widow has put in more than all who have contributed to the treasury; for they have all put in money they could spare, but she in her poverty has put in everything she possessed, all she had to live on" (Mk 12:41–44, NJB).

At bottom, and this is the third difficulty, donor recognition is quite simply biblically indefensible. Jesus could not have been clearer:

> Beware of practicing your piety before others in order to be seen by them; for then you have no reward from your Father in heaven. So whenever you give alms, do not sound a trumpet before you, as the hypocrites do in the synagogues and in the streets, so that they may be praised by others. Truly I tell you, they have received their reward. But when you give alms, do not let your left hand know what your right hand is doing, so that your alms may be done in secret; and your Father who sees in secret will reward you (Mt 6:1–6).

Jesus shows himself singularly uninterested in appearances or the regard of others. One gives alms because it is the right thing to do. Indeed not only are we to avoid publicity: we are actually to seek anonymity. It is the approval of God which matters, and God, "who sees in secret" will reward us.

Practically speaking, donor recognition programs also create habits that are nearly impossible to break. Once naming opportunities are introduced to a community of faith, members will not only see them as legitimate, but will rely upon them for future giving. It is almost impossible for a pastor or church board to tell a family that a large gift will not entitle them to a naming opportunity when this has been the practice of the community in the past. Such a situation will inevitably lead to uncomfortable and unavoidably divisive conflict.

A related problem is the permanence which is, or is not, understood to attach to naming opportunities. I have personally witnessed a local church offer to replace the memorial dedications on stained glass windows in an attempt to "sell" them as part of a new fundraising scheme. Not only did this cause pain to those families who originally dedicated the windows to their loved ones, but it acted to devalue the naming opportunity for the new "prospects" from whom the church tried to raise money. Several of the families that did "purchase" windows as a new naming opportunity for their loved ones actually negotiated with the Church Council, stating their apprehension that if they were able to "buy" windows that had previously been recognition items for other families, they had no reason to believe that the Council would not remove their own name in the future, thereby lowering the value of their gift. In the end, several church members who had previously dedicated windows to loved ones, and a number of their friends, left the church; the fundraising goal was not met; and the pastor's integrity was so compromised that he felt he had no choice but to ask for reassignment. The same has been true of "buy a brick" and other programs. Eventually, physical recognition programs become outdated by the need for renovations, expansion, demolition, or other such changes and interventions.

A Study in Donor Recognition

Naming opportunities as part of fundraising schemes are not new, and antiquity provides us a salutary example. In the fifth century C.E. a man by the name of Lampadius funded the refurbishment of the Amphitheatrum Flavium. We know this because he was recognized for his gift by the placement of a stone plaque in an entranceway to the Colosseum. Newly discovered physical evidence suggests that the very stone which recognizes Lampadius' gift was a mere four centuries earlier a donor recognition plaque for the Emperor Vespasian, who provided the money to renovate the Colosseum after Nero had bankrupted the empire, and burned Rome itself.[33]

---

[33] Louis H. Feldman suggests that the Lampadian stone carving was previously a donor recognition plaque thanking Vespasian for the funds used to renovate the Colosseum. Feldman argues that the money for the renovation was provided (unwillingly) by booty taken from the Jews and the Temple in the sacking of Jerusalem in 70 C.E. Feldman, "Financing the

Interesting ethical questions are raised by these examples of donor recognition in the Roman Colosseum. Where did Lampadius get his money? Is it acceptable to receive gifts from a man who has made his fortune through the oppression of others, or through an industry that is socially unacceptable? (Every indication is that Lampadius was a profiteer from the gladiatorial games which continued to persecute Christians, and showcase human death as entertainment, through the fifth century C.E.) And even if Lampadius' donation was "clean," what obligation did the Roman people have to sustain the name and memory of their initial patron, Vespasian?

And what about Vespasian? Was he the real donor, or did Vespasian receive credit for the bounty which the Empire was amassing through the subjugation of foreign nations? Was it legal or ethical to use money from the Jews as tribute to the polytheistic Roman society? And so on. Donor recognition clearly raises a host of questions and problems, many of which defy clear solution even from the vantage point of centuries' distance.

At its best, the principle underlying donor recognition is the sincere desire to show gratitude to those who are charitably generous. This is quite different from using rewards and recognition in order to pry money out of people. It is hardly surprising that when recognition is a substantial part of one's motive for giving, such that the gift is in some sense conditional upon an agreeable "reward," charitable organizations find

---

Colosseum," *Biblical Archaeology Review,* 27, no. 4 (2001): 22–31, 60–61. Feldman points out that this argument is given added weight by Josephus' account of the fall of the Temple, "so glutted with plunder were the troops, one and all, that throughout Syria the standard of gold was depreciated to half its former value" (Josephus: *Jewish Wars* 6.317). In addition, the so-called "Copper Scroll" discovered in Qumran's Cave 3 in 1952 lists the treasures of the Temple at the time of the destruction of the Temple and looting by the Romans.

themselves entangled in the strings attached to the gifts they
receive. This is the antithesis of stewardship, where gifts are given
freely, and for love of the other as oneself because of the "love
gift"—Jesus—whom God has freely given to us. If we believe that
our generosity is a sign of our own gratitude to God for the
abundance we enjoy, then our charitable gifts are more properly an
act of worship which is meant to "recognize" our Creator—not
ourselves. While secular fundraisers may promote donor
recognition as a successful means of encouraging giving, we
Christians must be true to our fundamental values as set forth in
Scripture and faith.

Gratitude is, of course, entirely appropriate: to withhold thanks
would be unthinkable. The Church is nothing if it is not a
community which places gratitude (the "Great Thanksgiving") at
the transformative center of its communal life. Such thanksgiving
however, is always meant to build up community, drawing us into
a more complete oneness, in which there is neither "Jew nor Greek,
slave nor free, male nor female," rich nor poor, major giver nor
general giver (after Gal 3:28). How we demonstrate our
appreciation to each other needs to incorporate these same
fundamentally *inclusive* values. And this can be quite simply and
fittingly done, through such means as personalized thank you
notes, communal celebration services, or any other creative means.

Certainly, let us give thanks for the generosity which is shown
to us—freely given thanks, for freely given gifts.

Chapter X
The Gift Chart –
Substituting Process for Values

From time to time, notwithstanding good ongoing stewardship, a Christian community may feel itself called to an extraordinary outlay of resources, and therefore, the need to conduct a financial campaign. For too long, churches in this position have been taught to make use of an "Essential Gifts Chart." The gift chart has its roots in secular fundraising, and is the method of choice for almost every financial campaign administered in universities, hospitals, libraries, and other secular charities. It is a dual purpose tool, which not only evaluates an organization's potential to raise money, but also sets out a method for doing so.

The use of the chart allows organizations easily to review their donor list to determine if they have the financial resources available to succeed in their fundraising efforts. The gift chart method is not concerned with the development of donors as stewards, and it is altogether silent on the subject of time and talent. One might well ask, "Then why would churches use it?" The rationale is simple, and regrettably, churches have fallen for it: the gift chart allows an organization to easily, quickly and efficiently estimate the *maximum* amount of money that may be available to it through the *minimum* effort possible.

How does the gift chart method work? First, a table is assembled based on a decades old "expert" assumption about how much money a church of a given size might reasonably seek to raise. In the following chart, the goal has been set at $500,000, and it is estimated that it would take a congregation of between 100–200 families to reach that goal. The rest of the chart is simple arithmetic. The gift chart implies that to raise any sum you must first find a single household to provide 20% of the goal. Then another three households must be found to provide another 30% of the goal; five more to provide another 10% (theoretically the amount raised is now at $300,000 or 60% of the goal from only nine households); and finally, an undetermined number of households are required to give smaller gifts until the congregation reaches its target.

A Sample Essential Gifts Chart
(For A Goal of $500,000 / A Church of 100–200 Families)

Size of Gift	# Needed	Cumulative Total
$100,000	1	$ 100,000
$ 75,000	1	$ 175,000
$ 50,000	1	$ 225,000
$ 25,000	1	$ 250,000
$ 10,000	5	$ 300,000
$ 5,000	10	$ 350,000
$ 3,000	25	$ 425,000
$ 1,000	50	$ 475,000
Below $ 1,000	Many	Goal Achieved

A formulaic method like the gift chart commends itself to secular fundraisers because it is easily implemented, requiring almost no special skill. It is process-driven: the unswerving adherence to a prescribed method will produce predictable outcomes. More than this, the gift chart method offers the promise of a high return on a relatively low investment of time and effort. There is not even the pretense of interest in developing a donor's sense of connection to the organization and/or community. Indeed, the gift chart is based upon the assumption that the organization does not *want* to invite every household to participate. Rather than treating all households equally, the objective is to raise a large amount of money from as few people as possible. The reason given for this is to allow the organization to return as quickly as it can to its "real mission," whether that is to provide medical care, access to books, the education of students, or whatever else.

The gift chart method is, therefore, fundamentally contrary to the Christian's understanding and values of good stewardship and community. It proceeds from the objectification of donors as possessors of wealth, and leaves aside any attempt to encourage personal commitment, faith or generosity—all key components of our vocational understanding of stewardship. In short, congregations cannot pursue resources through an objective methodology such as the gift chart, and expect Christian stewardship, a subjective value, in return.

Unfortunately, however, the gift chart has been used almost exclusively in mainline church financial campaigns for decades. In the late 1950s a fundraising firm that operated in both the United States and Canada successfully promoted this method as "the only model for Church fundraising." The way these campaigns were "pitched" appealed to these still rapidly growing churches. The gift chart method did not require a lot of volunteers, sought gifts from only a few households, and was quick. With no end in sight to mass immigration after World War II, and for churches worried about building quickly enough to meet their expanding needs, this method was, as it was promoted in its day, "… the financial salvation for a Church in need."[34]

The attraction of the gift chart method lay precisely in the fact that it was process-driven. It was easy to understand, and was naturally appealing to those individuals and communities who lacked stewardship skills. People knew exactly what was going to happen in Week One, Two or Three of the campaign, and if they did their work correctly, the outcome promised to be exactly what they expected. For secular fundraisers, who were used to implementing gift chart methodology in the secular non-profit sector, its adoption by the mainline churches opened up new markets for professional fundraising which had previously been inaccessible because of the special skills, pastoral understanding, faith, and commitment these churches needed and had heretofore expected and demanded of themselves. In the end, knowing how the gift chart method worked became a substitute for understanding the institutional church, faith and stewardship. And for North Americans who were welcoming electric toasters, self-cleaning ovens, and other conveniences that made life easy and care free, the gift chart matched their newly embraced values: it was efficient, time saving, and easy.

It is long past time, however, to revisit the gift chart method in light of our Christian values and convictions. Unfortunately, the financial "success" of these campaigns has become embedded in the collective memory of the faithful, leading many to conclude, mistakenly, that the gift chart model must therefore also be "good." Some evangelical churches in recent decades have also begun to take note of this method and have accepted its usefulness to a greater or lesser extent. Effective though the gift chart may be in the secular arena, it is utterly inappropriate for use in the Church.

---

[34] 1958 Marketing letter of the Wells Co., a fundraising firm that was active in the 1950s and 1960s.

True stewardship is a measure of more than dollars, and methods like the gift chart deprive the faithful of such other "goods" as community building, personal development and adherence to Gospel traditions.

One of the most glaring problems with the gift chart method is that it seizes upon objective criteria, such as wealth, rather than generosity, as a means of estimating and pursuing success. Not only does this cause the congregational leadership to objectify members in order to determine whether there are enough wealthy people to provide the majority of resources, but it forces them to make assumptions about people's individual means and willingness to contribute to the campaign. Such a process courts pastoral conflict because it entails, or is assumed to entail, a review of people's annual offerings—or it requires the leadership to make assumptions on the basis of information which may have been provided in different contexts, for different reasons. Members will quickly lose confidence in their leadership if they believe that their lives are being "evaluated" according to financial information, perceptions or assumptions. The gift chart method of fundraising fundamentally breaches the trust of members that their socio-economic status will have no bearing on their spiritual or religious worth to a community of faith.

Another problem with the gift chart model is that it relies too heavily upon the contributions of a few, rather than engaging the entire community. Consider again the use of a gift chart in a congregation of 100–200 households (*see* A Sample Essential Gifts Chart on p. 102). As stated, according to this method, the congregation would expect to rely upon only 9 households for 60% of its total funding need. With barely 5% of the congregation providing 60% of the goal, the congregation is sending a strong signal to 95% of members that the responsibility to provide financial resources for ministry, worship and outreach belongs to "someone else." When we employ this model the congregation becomes fragmented. The majority of members are actually being taught to believe that stewardship is not their personal responsibility. Meanwhile, the wealthy few who are "targeted" by the gift chart method are invariably left embittered and wondering, "Why don't others give?" In the end, members are formed to take part in "institutional welfare," where it is possible for a majority to coast on the benevolence of those few who are believed to have greater resources at their disposal. The problem with this is that it discourages any real sense of shared ownership in a community project—and this includes a shared desire to pay for its ongoing maintenance and renewal. This is not stewardship. It belies our ancient values that everyone is capable of being generous, no matter how poor he or she may be. Moreover, once a congregation learns this model, and is formed in its ways, it is extremely hard to let it go. Because real change is generally slow and incremental, it can take a whole generation to unlearn and supplant what the previous generation held as good and valuable.

Another failing of the gift chart method is its total inattention to the corollary benefits of a congregational campaign. Stewardship and financial campaigns present a wonderful opportunity for members to meet each other, to build community, and to encourage good stewardship. The fact that the gift chart method engages so few people for personal visits, coupled with fundraisers' tendency to assign these visits to the pastor and other leaders, means that the majority of members will not take part in the campaign either as a visitor, or as one who is visited. Consequently ownership of the campaign and the shared responsibility and value of stewardship are lost.

Gift chart based campaigns also proceed on the unsustainable assumption that all congregations are the same. The success of the gift chart method is predicated on every congregation having 5% of its households affluent enough, and willing, to provide for the majority of the financial goal (that is, donors who both can and will). It defies reason that the economic demography of every congregation is identical, or that even if it was, all members would give in a predictably like manner. The imposition of a gift chart formula on rural, small, or poor congregations can defeat even the most enthusiastic of dreams. It should be noted that such congregations are often entirely capable of raising the funds they need using a model more consonant with our Christian values. But, not surprisingly, once presented with the daunting task of finding several wealthy donors to underwrite the bulk of the goal, they often give up before they even start. The use of the gift chart method is quite simply inappropriate to evaluate a congregation's ability to raise money, and is wholly inadvisable for Christian use at all in fundraising or stewardship campaigns.

Even worse, because the gift chart method does not promote ownership of stewardship as a personal value amongst members, congregations that use it find themselves having to implement campaigns on an increasingly frequent basis. When members do not respond to God's call to stewardship as part of their ongoing Christian vocation, communities lapse repeatedly into crisis, and financial campaigns are required to provide the resources for ministry. Unfortunately, once gift chart methodology is fixed in the experience and expectations of the faithful, the congregation falls into an endless loop of campaigning to keeping its head above water, expending the majority of its time, talent, and treasure seeking time, talent, and treasure. This is a strategy for survival, not for mission.

If the Christian community is to provide the resources it needs to undertake the work to which all Christians are called, then we have to go beyond gift charts and invite members to be stewards. Only stewardship will encourage all people to be open-handed with their time, talents, and treasure, in order that Christians, both individually and organizationally, may respond to God's call. The gift chart method may be easy, but expediency makes a poor god. Our future lies not in gift charts, but in the values inherent in our Christian faith.

Chapter XI
What We Sow So Shall We Reap—
Counting on Major Gifts to Save Us

One feature of secular fundraising which is currently receiving a great deal of emphasis is the solicitation of "major gifts" and corporate giving. Major gift campaigns effectively exploit and perpetuate current patterns in philanthropic giving, but for reasons we shall make clear, when imported into churches and Christian organizations are a highly counter-productive influence in the development of healthy stewardship.

Most people are familiar with the celebrated foundations and trusts that bear the names of the "robber baron" wealthy—the Rockefeller Foundation, the Carnegie Endowment, the Beaverbrook Foundation, and the host of others that continue to do great works of charity across the continent. However, impressive though the charitable works of these foundations may be, the truth is that the largest source of charitable giving in North America is still donations by individuals.

In 1996, individuals were responsible for fully 80% of all charitable giving in the United States.[35] Of the $150 billion in

---

[35] Based on Melissa S. Brown, ed., "1998 Revised Estimate of All Charitable Contributions," *Giving USA 2001* (Indianapolis: AAFRC Trust for Philanthropy, 2001), p. 156, and taking account of reports by the IRS indicating an additional $28 billion in estimated contributions by non-

philanthropic donations, $120 billion was given by individuals. By 2000, individual charitable gifts had risen to an unprecedented $152.07 billion. And yet, despite a robust economy, this amount accounted for only 75% of the national total, which had increased to $203.45 billion. This represents a decline of 5%.[36] Notwithstanding an increased focus and investment in philanthropy, individual giving is thus showing all the signs of lagging behind philanthropic giving as a whole.

In Canada, total direct financial support to charitable and non-profit organizations totaled an estimated $4.51 billion in 1996[37] (3% of total charitable giving in the United States during the same period). Even adjusted for population, Canadian philanthropic giving was only 27.8% of the American total in the same year. This is not to say that Canadians are not generous. While the number of dollars given is remarkably different than in the United States, Canadians are becoming increasingly charitable.[38] Indeed, the growth in the fledgling Canadian philanthropic sector shows that

---

itemizing taxpayers.

[36] *Ibid.*

[37] Source: Statistics Canada, *NSGVP Highlights,* Catalogue no. 71-542-XIE, 1997, p. 10.

[38] It is almost impossible to draw direct comparisons between philanthropic giving in the United States and Canada. However, the general trends are the same in both countries. Individuals account for the most significant portion of philanthropic giving, and the upward trend of generosity amongst lower income groups increased overall giving to religious causes and programs historically administered by the State. It is my contention that just as the Church lost its sense of stewardship wherever it was "established" or became an agent of the State, so has government sponsorship of social services made Canadians more willing to pay higher taxes, but less inclined than Americans to give directly to philanthropic causes.

Canadians are individually willing to take up needs currently being transferred from the State to private, public and religious charities.

Individual Philanthropic Giving
United States versus Canada
Comparing 1996 & 2000

United States

	Total Charitable $	Total by Individuals	% of Giving	% to Religious	Avg. Annual Gift
1996	$150 billion	$120 billion	80%	46%	$1,009 (US)
2000	$203.45 billion	$152.07 billion	75%	36.5%	$1,620 (US)

Canada

	Total Charitable $	Total by Individuals	% of Giving	% to Religious	Avg. Annual Gift
1996	$4.51 billion	$3.52 billion	78%	52%	$239 (CAN)
2000	$5 billion	$3.9 billion	78%	49%	$259 (CAN)

Statistics reveal troubling similarities between the two countries. First, charitable giving to religious causes has sharply decreased in the past five years, down from 46% in 1996 amongst Americans, to 36.5% in 2000 (a decline of 9.5%),[39] and down 3%

---

[39] *Giving USA, 2001*, p. 34.

overall amongst Canadians.[40] There is greater competition for philanthropic dollars, and it seems as if churches are being neglected in favor of social services and the arts. Second, the trend toward fewer, but larger, gifts has been markedly rising in both countries. The Canadian Centre for Philanthropy notes:

> The average annual donation in 2000 increased by 8% from 1997, to $259. Canadian donors made fewer, but larger individual donations in 2000...[41]

Consider the chart "Distribution of Charitable Giving By Income Levels (U.S.)" for 1995, 1997 and 1999.[42] Clearly, it is middle income Americans (those making between $30,000 and $75,000) who provide the vast majority of philanthropic dollars. However, during the 1990s, despite the longest period of economic growth in American history, this same group registered a 10% decline in their share of the total raised (from 56% to 46%).

By contrast, those earning between $75,000 and $200,000 increased their share of the total donated to charity. Moreover, by 1999, the very wealthiest Americans accounted for 6% of total givings, whereas they had contributed only 4% of the total in 1995. Given that those in the highest income brackets comprise a much smaller pool of donors than low and middle income earners, these increases are pointed evidence of fundraisers' growing emphasis

---

[40] Based on a comparison of Marcus Parmegiani, "Charitable Giving in Canada: Fact Sheet, 1997" (Toronto: Canadian Centre for Philanthropy, 2002), p. 3–4, and Fleur Leslie, "Charitable Giving in Canada, 2000" (Toronto: CCP, 2002), p. 3.

[41] Source: Statistics Canada, *NSGVP Highlights,* Catalogue no. 71-542-XIE, 2000, p. 10.

[42] "Statistics of Income Bulletin, Spring 1997, 1999, 2001" (Washington, D.C.: Internal Revenue Service, 2001).

on major gifts—gifts, that is, which are only within the reach of the wealthy. Major gift campaigns are causing a shift in the patterns of charitable giving, by de-emphasizing or even ignoring the generosity of the vast majority of willing givers, simply because they have less disposable income to share.

Distribution of Charitable Giving By Income Levels (U.S.)				
Adjusted Gross Income	**1995**	**1997**	**1999**	**Trend**
Under $20,000	1%	5%	7%	↑
$20,000 – $30,000	13%	8%	7%	↓
$30,000 – $50,000	26%	23%	20%	↓
$50,000 – $75,000	30%	28%	26%	↓
$75,000 – $100,000	14%	17%	17%	→
$100,000 – $200,000	12%	14%	17%	↑
$200,000 – Over	4%	5%	6%	↑

The attraction of "targeting" corporations and the wealthy is understandable. Secular fundraisers go after major gifts because this allows an organization to reach its goal with the least expenditure of effort possible. Major gifts are, in business terms, cost-effective. The same culture of crass commercialism that promotes the pursuit of big gifts consequently has little use for encouraging support from the broadest spectrum of people. It is just too much work, and too expensive, for the return expected on the fundraising dollar.

Unfortunately, this increased reliance on major gifts is self-perpetuating. In his landmark critique of welfare and the Great

Society, United States Senator Daniel Patrick Moynihan pointed out that the more you subsidize something, the more of it you will experience. It is not surprising then that secular fundraisers' pursuit of major gifts produces not only more major gifts, but an ever increasing emphasis on major gift campaigns. The trouble is that this occurs at the cost of middle income philanthropy—which ought to be valued not only for the gifts to be received, but for the widely shared act of philanthropy itself.

Moreover, the confidence fundraisers place in major gift donors is based upon flawed assumptions. The idea that wealthy people will give to philanthropic causes simply because they can afford to, or that wealthy people are chiefly responsible for the philanthropic heart of North America, is wholly without merit. Statistically, those of the lowest income brackets are far more generous with their resources than the wealthy. The philanthropic sector in Canada is proof positive of this assertion. Atlantic Canada, including Newfoundland, Prince Edward Island (PEI), Nova Scotia and New Brunswick are amongst the poorest of Canada's ten provinces. However, these provinces have traditionally held the distinction of having the highest donor participation rates in Canada, even outdistancing Ontario, by far Canada's wealthiest province.[43]

Likewise, statistics show lower income Americans to be increasingly philanthropically inclined. A review of the chart previously cited, "Distribution of Charitable Giving by Income Levels" (p. 112) shows that the percentage contributed by lower income Americans actually grew, more than quintupling in less than five years. In other words, the most significant growth in philanthropic giving took place amongst the poorest of Americans, often those most in need of philanthropic dollars themselves. To

---

[43] Adapted from Statistics Canada, *NSGVP Highlight,* Catalogue no. 71-542-XIE, 1997, pp. 54,56,58,60,64.

ignore lower income givers is not only contrary to our Christian values and understanding of generosity as taught in the story of 'the widow's mite' (Mk 12:41–44) but, in the vulgar phrase of secular fundraisers, "leaves money on the table."

Donor Participation Rate: Atlantic Canada

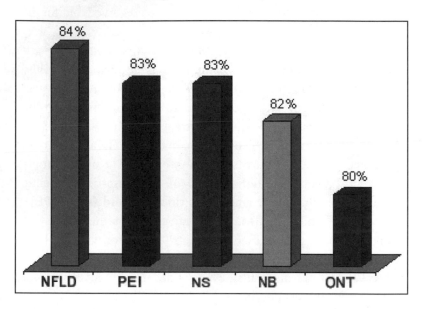

For the Christian community, the pursuit of major gifts from the wealthy can lead to other extremely unhealthy trends in congregations. The issue is not merely that secular fundraising fails to engage everyone. The pursuit of major gifts also overlooks gifts of time and talent. While it has been established that there is a significant connection between volunteering and financial offerings, what is little spoken of is that this trend does not hold true for upper income earners. The fact is that the wealthier people become, the less likely they are to volunteer. The interrelatedness of the giving of time and talent to the gift of treasure, and the converse, indicates that, with the exception of the wealthy, those most likely to give are also more likely to volunteer. The corollary is also true, as evidenced by the Maritime provinces' disproportionate rate of volunteerism amongst Canadians in general. In other words, good stewardship occurs more often amongst the poor than the wealthy. If offerings are lagging in churches it is most likely tied to a decrease in volunteer ministry amongst middle and lower income earners. If we believe Christ when he taught, "Where your treasure is there your heart will be also" (Mt 6:21), then the pursuit of major gifts from the well-to-do may not only diminish giving amongst other church members, but may have the unintended consequence of diminishing volunteer involvement in ministry as well.

The obsession with major gifts also ignores the philanthropic will and generosity of particular ethnic and religious communities, who tend to be disproportionately represented amongst lower income households. According to research conducted by Independent Sector, Hispanics and African-Americans are rapidly growing segments of the community who engage in philanthropic causes. Almost "63% of Hispanic households gave to charity in 1998, representing an increase of 6 percentage points over 1995 figures (57%),"[44] each making an average gift of $504. In the same year, the average contribution to charity by African-Americans was $658.[45]

While fundraisers may point to the fact that white residents gave an average of $1,174,[46] churches should take note that the

---

[44] William A. Diaz *et al.*, "Hispanic Giving and Volunteering: Findings from Independent Sector's National Survey of Giving and Volunteering," *Facts and Findings* 3, no. 3 (Washington, D.C.: Independent Sector, 2001), p. 1.

[45] Independent Sector, "The Demographics of Household Contributors and Volunteers," *Giving and Volunteering* (1999).

[46] *Ibid.*

majority of donations by African-Americans and Hispanics are directed to religious causes[47]—not only because churches are the beneficiary of this generosity, but because as Christians we have a moral obligation to help dispel age-old biases that have discounted the real contribution of these communities. The truth is that the disparity in the level of giving relates not only to relative income (a smaller gift may well be a more generous one), but to the fact that no one asked. Sadly, and too often, these ethnic groups are not even invited to participate in philanthropy because of an unworthy and untested assumption that they would not. In fact, however, when asked, Hispanics gave and volunteered as generously as non-Hispanics, and demonstrated an increase in volunteer participation from 40% in 1995, to 46% in 1998. When asked, Hispanics are just as likely to volunteer as white people.[48]

Ethnicity is not the only factor that is generally overlooked in the pursuit of major gifts (and charitable giving in general, for that matter). As previously noted, religious practices and attendance at worship are primary factors in philanthropic generosity. Nearly all donations by Southerners and "born again" Christians, for instance, are given in the pews.[49]

The issue of evangelical giving patterns, particularly as this relates to the tithe, provides an interesting sidebar. To be sure, evangelical Christians are disproportionately generous when compared to most Americans, and indeed when compared to most churchgoers. In 1999, the average level of charitable giving for

---

[47] Jennifer Lach, "Divine Interventions," *American Demographics Magazine*, June, 2000.

[48] Diaz, "Hispanic Giving and Volunteering," *Giving and Volunteering,* 1998.

[49] Lach, *Idem.*

those who described themselves as churchgoers was $2,151.[50] Evangelical Christians gave 10% more, with an average gift of $2,346.[51]

However, those denominations who look with envy at the evangelical "tithe" should note that while (only) 32% of evangelical Christians claim to tithe, an even smaller percentage, 12%, actually do.[52] Indeed, in 2000 alone, evangelical Christians gave 16% less in absolute dollars than they did in 1999.[53] The introduction of the tithe, or simple "proportional giving," will not be the panacea some suppose to the need for financial resources.

Not least this is because, for Christians, generosity is the principal criterion by which to measure philanthropy. Note that if an individual earning $20,000 per annum were to make gifts of 7% to their church and other Christian ministries, this would amount to $1,400. For an upper income earner ($200,000 and above), gifts of only 5% would produce $10,000. It is easy to see why fundraisers "target the upper income." Yet, while a wealthy household will scarcely feel the impact of a $10,000 gift, especially if they are able to turn it to their tax-advantage, $1,400 for a poor household is likely a third of their annual food budget. Note then that proportional gifts, like major gifts, are not necessarily generous or sacrificial.

When a congregation falls into the habit of pursuing and receiving major gifts at the expense of promoting stewardship, it generally fails to appreciate the willing generosity that may come

---

[50] Independent Sector, *Giving and Volunteering, Key Findings,* 2001.

[51] Lach, *Idem.*

[52] Barna Research Ltd, cited by Generous Giving, "Giving by Evangelical Christian Americans," *Giving Statistics* (Generous Giving: 2001), p. 2.

[53] *Ibid.*

from the sacrifice of lower-income households. This is not to say that major gifts are bad. Indeed, if the promotion of Christian generosity were taken more seriously, churches and Christian organizations would receive many more "major gifts" than they do, since wealthy Christians would give in proportion to their income. But major gifts should be the outcome of a generous heart, not the product of a well researched and practiced "ask" for money.

Congregations which rely heavily on major gifts often see an imbalance in their offerings, akin to the frequently cited phenomenon of 20% of the people giving 80% of the resources. This is the dynamic we have called "institutional welfare," whereby the majority of members learn to rely upon the few to provide resources for the entire congregation. Aside from the lack of vocational stewardship development amongst the whole People of God, a number of other problems ensue:

- congregations cease to take ownership of the responsibility for good stewardship, and it is left to the pastor and a small circle of congregational leaders to take charge, and to provide the time required to meet the community's financial needs
- the majority of members learn to expect someone else to provide resources
- should the congregation rely upon a major gift donor who subsequently leaves the community through death, departure, or dissatisfaction, there will be a need to find an equally willing and wealthy members to fill the void
- a "power dynamic" is initiated, whereby major gift donors expect the pastor and congregational leadership to consult with them, and take direction proportionate to their giving
- since fewer donors provide the majority of resources and therefore feel "ownership" of the programs supported, contributions from other members of the community begin to fall off

It is evident that secular fundraisers who have worked in churches and Christian ministries have been "forming" individuals and the organizations themselves to value major gifts. In so doing, we have imitated the secular arena, by devaluing regular and general philanthropy, especially amongst middle income earning households. There is a causal connection between secular fundraisers' obsession with major gifts, and the general decline in the participation and level of generosity in philanthropy in general.

If people do not learn the love of humanity (philanthropy) from the churches, then surely they will emulate what they experience in society. This does not bode well for the churches, Christian ministries or society as a whole. Archbishop William Temple, a former Archbishop of Canterbury, was right when he declared that the Church is the only institution that exists for the sake of those who do not belong to it. In this sense, we have an obligation not just to ourselves, but to society itself, to stem the tide of poor stewardship, and to embrace and enact values that are not only those of our Christian faith, but which are compatible with good citizenship. For the sake of the Body of Christ, and the world "God so loved" we must recover Christian stewardship from secular fundraising without delay.

Chapter XII
Start Your Stewardship Renewal Program Without Asking for Money

Recognizing the need to recover Christian stewardship from the deleterious impact of secular fundraising is one thing. Actually recommitting one's congregation and Christian ministry to stewardship renewal is another. What, then, are some practical steps to begin liberating the congregation or organization, the faithful, and our tired old practices from the treadmill of fundraising and secularism?

Christian stewardship embraces every aspect of our lives and our giftedness. It cannot be reduced to money and the management of our financial resources alone, but is rather triune in nature—time, talent, and treasure. If we are going to renew our understanding of stewardship as a matter of Christian vocation, individually, at the congregational level, and at the level of the wider Christian ministries, we shall have to begin by restoring time and talent to their proper place. Moreover, statistics and experience confirm that time and talent properly *precede* treasure in the exercise of stewardship, so that any stewardship renewal program needs to treat time, talent and treasure in precisely that order.

The most powerful argument for this position is that it makes sense. To reflexively throw money at a problem without first understanding the underlying issues which give rise to it is irresponsible. We may take a lesson from the business world. (Not all business practices are automatically irrelevant or inappropriate for churches). No business person would make an outlay of resources without first evaluating both what is needed, and what is on hand. Individuals, and the Christian community as a whole, must assess how their time, talent, and treasure are currently being used before seeking or expending more time, talent, and treasure. Otherwise, dealing creatively with problems and challenges takes a back seat to raising money—the very problem which has brought the Christian community to its current crisis of stewardship. Once people have reviewed both what they have *contributed* of their time and talent, and how it has actually been *received* by churches and Christian ministries, then, and only then, does it make sense for them to entertain how much more of their time and talent they might give. Churches and Christian ministries also need to engage in this same reflection. Only once these issues have been addressed, and remediated if necessary, does it make sense to consider how much treasure might be needed to fund those ministries to which the individual and the church or organization have mutually agreed to commit their time and talent.

Stewardship renewal is akin to spiritual growth: it is cumulative and inductive by nature. In your growth in faith journey, you don't just learn *about* prayer, for example—you pray. But more than this, you begin a lifetime of growth in prayer. While most people begin by learning their bedtime and meal prayers, it is possible to advance as far as piety may allow. Similarly, stewardship renewal must be both educational and experiential. One learns to be a steward by practicing stewardship, and the life of the steward is characterized by progression and growth. Rarely does a sacrificial gift of material resources precede a commitment first of time, and next, of one's gifts and talents. Only once we have invested our *selves* in some cause are we prepared to "put our money where our mouth is."

Moreover, although stewardship is a matter for individual Christians, it cannot be thought of or practiced in a vacuum: like faith itself, it is a vocation to be worked out with, and within, the whole Body of Christ, the Church. Our faith journey and vocation as stewards is incomplete and unfulfilled outside of the community of faith, which teaches, and challenges, and needs us.

This said, stewardship renewal does not require top-down sponsorship. It can begin anywhere within the Body of Christ, and just as blood flows throughout the whole body, stewardship will as well, renewing each part of the Body as it flows.

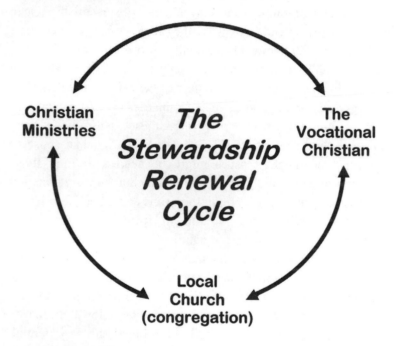

For practical reasons, however, I recommend that stewardship renewal begin at the congregational level. Most of us have little or no control over what the wider Body of Christ does: by focusing our attention where we can have real, meaningful, and widespread interaction, we are most able to effect change. A word of caution, however, since expectation management is important: real change is never expedient, and is always incremental. We will not be able to recover Christian stewardship from secular fundraising overnight. This, however, is not license to take our sweet time. It will take years to undo the damage which has been done, and we must delay no longer in setting about our task.

Reviewing our Individual Habits

Within the context of our congregational life, we may begin by reviewing our personal stewardship of *time*. I often begin training sessions by asking people to examine their appointment diaries. A date book can reveal a great deal about what is truly important to us. For instance, the person who spends a morning each week at a drop-in center for the homeless demonstrates a concern for the disadvantaged. The executive who protects time for his family may well have done so at the cost of other rewards. The individual who makes time for continuing education has chosen to care for the curiosity which God gave her. And so on. There is no better place to begin a personal evaluation of one's stewardship than to review one's calendar.

Christians who understand their vocation as stewards also engage in reflection about the use of their *talents*. Talents are the most wonderful of gifts simply because everyone has them. Whether obvious or hidden, we are called to discern our talents and put them to use in building up the Kingdom of God. Be it the ability to use calligraphy to create lovely cards and signs, the gift of a beautiful voice to praise God in worship, the talent of working patiently with children as they learn the complexity of their faith, or our education as writers, teachers, accountants, administrators and even lawyers—we all have talents. Sometimes our gifts fit easily into the needs our congregation has identified: a lawyer volunteers her time as a mediator for a peace and justice program, a teacher volunteers as a Sunday school teacher, or an administrative specialist uses his knowledge of software and computer systems to create the congregation's bulletin. Longtime married couples can be good counselors to young couples for retreats; a carpenter can refurbish a broken pew; a handi-worker can create banners for the liturgy; and many other gifts can be offered for the good of the Christian community. Some of these talents are as simple as being very personable, and able to greet seekers, searchers, adherents and members warmly as they arrive for worship. No talent should be ignored by the worshiper who *gives,* or by the congregation, which *receives.*

Having reached a conclusion about what kind of steward one is today, it is salutary to examine current needs, and to ask what is being demanded of us for the future. It is important to note that the exercise of Christian stewardship is not confined to the activities of the congregation, or even to faith-based projects. Community programs always need volunteers—for instance, cooks for the soup-kitchens, or visitors to shut-ins. Youth groups need leaders; choirs need singers; parks need conservators. Countless needs can be met through the gift of time and talent.

Within the congregation itself, there are many opportunities to match our abilities with identified needs. Church bulletin boards, newsletters and Sunday bulletins are all promising places to look. Here, indeed, we see the intersection between the individual and the congregation in the exercise of Christian stewardship, since the congregation must effectively and continuously convey its needs to the faithful. This conjunction between the needs and gifts of individuals, congregations, and/or the wider Christian community propels us all into a cycle of good stewardship.

The Church Community

The best congregational stewardship renewal program will be inductive, in that it actually engages people in the practice of stewardship, but—perhaps surprisingly—it will probably *not* be about stewardship itself. For obvious reasons, congregational seminars on the need for money or volunteers are pretty much non-starters. Nobody wants to be harangued. But more than this, people will not give to the church just because it needs money—or time, or talent. They will only give if they care about what the church does with their gift, if they believe that the church is engaged in something that *matters*. And here is the key to stewardship renewal.

Our best course of action is to identify some emergent issue or problem (it could be absolutely anything), and to invite people who have related interest or expertise to deal with it. What we are asking for, therefore, is a commitment of time, and of talent. We are asking for a wise assessment of the resources already at the disposal of the community, and the use it has made of them to date. Should this group of people then determine that money would be a productive solution to the stated problem, we can be assured of their exemplary commitment to that solution. As we have seen, statistics show that those who give freely of their time and talent to the church or other Christian ministry are also the most generous financial givers. This makes sense, for Jesus' proclamation that "where your treasure is, there your heart will be also" (Mt 6:21), is also true in the inverse: "where your heart is, so also will be your treasure." The point is this, that when we draw people into the management, or stewardship, of congregational life, they quite naturally become better and more conscientious stewards.

Consider the following scenario, and the fourfold problem-solving mechanism outlined in the following chart, where something as unanticipated as a comment from a visitor to the church becomes the starting point for a stewardship renewal program.

Problem Solving Mechanism

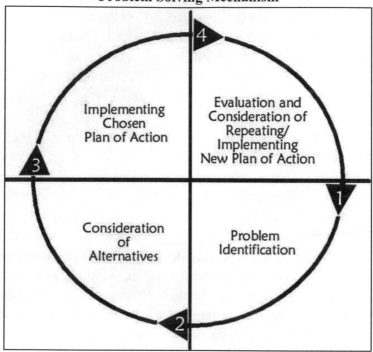

Scenario

One Sunday, a newcomer greets you at the back of the church following the service, and says, "I've driven by here a dozen times, but never came in until today because it didn't look inviting." You ask why, and are told, "The old style Gothic lettering on the sign made me think that this was a church stuck in the past, and I didn't want to join a dying congregation."

Following this interchange, you decide to walk around the building, and realize for the first time that the building you worship in every Sunday, with its parapets, Gothic construction, Old English lettered sign, and siege-proof wooden doors, is indeed uninviting, if not downright forbidding. You decide that something must be done. You also realize that you have an opportunity to engage other members of the congregation in this problem in such a way as to enhance and develop stewardship (Step 1: Problem Identification).

You thus begin your stewardship renewal program by gathering a few members you believe have something meaningful to contribute to the issue at hand. You ask these people to be part of an informal discussion: a long-time member, a new family, an architect, a graphic artist, and a landscaper. Not all have equal expertise, but they do represent all stakeholders, and you want to give them voice.

Together this group reaches the same conclusion you did, that the exterior of the church building is uninviting. However, the group disagrees as to what should or could be done. The group decides to present its concerns to the Church Council, which also concurs that something must be done.

The Church Council appoints the architect and landscaper to develop a report concerning the condition and visual aspects of the building exterior. Meanwhile, the graphic artist, a long-time member and a new worshiper begin to develop sketches of a new sign, and to research its cost. (This is Step 2: the Consideration of Alternatives.)

For now you decide that the visual impediments of the building will take a long time to remedy. In the interim you determine to make a new commitment to welcoming those visitors and potential members who do brave the foreboding exterior to give your church a try. You institute a series of training seminars and theological discussions about hospitality. This leads your ushers and greeters finally to feel valued and taken seriously, and they now respond with renewed enthusiasm to their ministry of welcoming seekers, searchers and visitors (Step 3: Implementing a Chosen Plan of Action).

Note how even before the solution to these problems has been fully implemented, you have begun your stewardship renewal program in a meaningful way: you have valued people's time and talents—both of which society frequently treasures over money. In the end, not only will you solve some of the problems that have contributed to your decline in church attendance. You will have celebrated the gifts of your members by asking them to be generous with them for the betterment of the Body of Christ. The excitement spilling out of a project as simple as this can be truly infectious, allowing you to address many other issues in the congregation, engaging even more members' time and talent.

It is at this point, when the congregation is ignited with hope from the generosity of time and talent flowing through it, that it can consider its next steps (Step 4: Evaluation and Consideration of Repeating the Plan of Action, or Implementing a New Plan). Out of this process of stewardship renewal, whether coincidentally or, preferably, by design, the congregation will embrace a vision of how it can best serve Christ and the community. With this newly embraced vision in hand, and a renewed sense of the true nature of stewardship, a congregation can begin to assess the financial resources it may need to implement the entire vision. Only at this point would a capital campaign or offerings campaign meet with success. Members will see that the days of treasure being sought as the substitute for true stewardship are over, and they will respond accordingly.

Chapter XIII
The Annual "Stewardship" Appeal –
Method vs. Values

It should be clear by now that the best plan for promoting congregational stewardship is constant immersion in our vocation to the Christian way of life—a vocation which has at its core a unique and individual conversion to the fullness of passionate stewardship. Within this larger context, however, will fall particular "stewardship" programs which may be more limited in scope. The "annual appeal," for example, tends to be strictly oriented to providing for the *financial* needs of the church. In this sense, although our treasure is one aspect of our total stewardship, the annual appeal is distinguishable from a true "stewardship" appeal. Such appeals, however, are a staple of congregational life, and as such, need to conform as fully as possible to the principles of good stewardship. Here, as elsewhere, however, the church has learned its methods and imbibed its assumptions from secular models. This brings us first, to a critical assessment of the secular preoccupation with cost-effectiveness, and second, to a description and appraisal of the annual appeal programs most commonly undertaken by the church.

Cost-Effectiveness and Stewardship
Secular fundraising methods continue to be driven by cost-effectiveness, with the consequence that profit may eclipse values

in the choices that are made. Regrettably, this is understandable, in view of the fact that a typical measure of a charity's "worthiness" of support is the ratio of administrative costs (including fundraising) to income—thereby putting pressure upon charities and fundraisers alike to keep costs low while maximizing return. Worse yet, there is really no uniform method by which costs can be allocated to either administration or program, with the result that comparisons between charities are not even equable. It is a perverse consequence of the need to show cost-effectiveness that the creativity of a charitable organization's accountants has a great deal to do with the "worthiness" rating it might receive.

This criticism is not to suggest that the economical management and deployment of resources is not a commendable goal: it is certainly one aspect of good stewardship. However, "economy" must be balanced against the kind of avarice that prevents us from lavishly placing such talents and resources as we possess to good use. (This is the message inherent in Jesus' parable of the talents, cf. Mt 25:14–29.) Moreover, not all the benefits of our philanthropy are monetary. An over-focus on cost-containment fundamentally undermines small charities whose mission may address a need not yet in the mainstream, or whose work may quite simply be superior in some way to that of larger organizations. The value to society of such a charity can easily outweigh any additional administrative cost.

The principles of Christian stewardship add another layer of criticism to our preoccupation with cost-effectiveness. Consider the annual bake sale. If one were to add up the cost of ingredients and figure in an hourly wage for the bakers, the proceeds of the bake sale would make it a meritless fundraising activity. The same could be said of the annual rummage sale (in my church, people bring such deplorable items that this event is fondly known as the "Junk for Jesus" sale), which is a lot of work, for a lot of people, for relatively little money. But real stewardship isn't just about money. Events like a bake sale or bazaar have all sorts of corollary benefits: not least is the gift of time and talent which they invite, the leadership and organizational skills which they develop, the sense of community which is built, the opportunity for the congregation to connect with its neighbors, and so on. Any effort which is narrowly focused on money, or which strives to use as few volunteers as possible, is antithetical at the level of first principles to Christian stewardship. This is not to say that bake sales and car washes can, or ought, ever to replace the ongoing congregational stewardship program; but it is to protect their place as augmentations to the broader plan, and as significant opportunities to promote the generous giving and gracious reception of time, talent and treasure.

It is important that we keep our first principles at the forefront of their decision-making about stewardship. To the extent that Christians have been seduced by the secular obsession with implementing the most resource-free and cost-effective fundraising practices available, and intertwined them into our own stewardship practices, we have come to behave as if we believe that cost-effective means "good." Yet, no church can claim to be truly cost-effective: the cost of maintaining our buildings and paying our pastors is almost always higher than the costs associated with the ministry, program and witness the church provides. To thus conclude that the church is not "worthy" of charitable support would be ludicrous. The truth is that cost-effectiveness sometimes gets in the way of fairly evaluating a charity's worth, and always of assessing the worth of the Body of Christ, to whom God has entrusted the ministration of the very most priceless of treasures—redemption in Christ Jesus.

Annual Financial Programs

It is this larger and sacred mission to minister Christ to the world that lays upon us the need for adequate and stable revenue, and which leads many churches to engage in some type of annual financial appeal. For this reason I believe it useful to review some of the more common plans and programs to encourage people to give their treasure in support of the mission and ministry of their local church. The brief critique of each of these programs should not be considered exhaustive, nor strictly stewardship based, but rather includes both secular and stewardship centered criticisms.

Impersonal Approaches

Few congregations engage in purely impersonal approaches to financial appeals, and some—particularly amongst the historic mainline churches—not at all. However, such appeals are implemented by some communities, and are certainly standard practice in the secular charitable arena. Some of these approaches have included:

Direct Mail Appeal

In a direct mail appeal, an organization mails letters to its "donor base" describing its current financial needs, and asking for a financial declaration (pledge) by return post. A church is more likely to get a high rate of return using this method than secular charities, although the return is only marginally higher. Most members take seriously the idea that they belong to a community of faith, and therefore do not respond well to highly impersonal bulk mailings. Some churches have attempted, with uneven success, to improve their rate of return by personalizing the salutation, or by adding handwritten messages to the standard letter. Experience shows that churches which choose a direct mail appeal as their primary method of eliciting annual financial declarations (pledges) are rarely concerned with either creativity and/or personalization, however. Some churches restrict the use of direct mail solicitation to specific appeals, most especially at year's end, in the event of a financial shortfall. The greatest problem with this approach, aside from its impersonal nature, is how few people actually follow through and return their pledge cards, whether by mail, or by delivering them personally to the church and dropping them into the collection plate.

SOME DIRECT MAIL APPEAL MERITS:
- Requires only a small number of people to administer
- Can be quickly implemented
- Allows financial needs to be distilled into a single, clear, concise, and uniform message

SOME DIRECT MAIL APPEAL CONCERNS:
- Highly impersonal
- Few people open direct mailings, even from their own church
- Precludes a discussion of issues of concern to members and adherents
- Can be costly, especially when a congregational list has not been routinely updated
- Response rates tend to be less than 20%
- Lack of personal appeal undermines the important nature of stewardship

Telephone Canvass Appeal

One might expect that a canvass by telephone would satisfy the escalating complaints of donors that they have little time to spare for philanthropic appeals. However, the inability of callers actually to connect with a significant number of people by telephone is quickly making this an obsolete method of conducting an annual financial appeal. Technologies such as answering machines, voice mail, caller identification, and call screening all create virtual impediments to what are essentially telemarketing campaigns. Further, without access to a single room (call center) in which telephone canvassers (telemarketers) can be supported, supervised, and encouraged, it is unlikely that callers will devote the time and attention required to make a telephone canvass appeal "successful." Finally, in almost all studies of the philanthropic sector, supporters are citing increased irritation at having their personal time interrupted by impersonal appeals for money. There is no indication that church members are any more welcoming of such appeals.

SOME TELEPHONE CANVASS APPEAL MERITS:
- Alleviates canvassers' anxiety about asking for money personally

SOME TELEPHONE CANVASS APPEAL CONCERNS:
- Highly impersonal
- Requires numerous attempts, and much time, to make live connection with members
- When messages are left, it shifts the responsibility to members to return the telephone call
- Likely to reach families at inopportune times
- People don't like discussing money over the telephone
- Requires a significant amount of training for the telephone canvassers
- Does not necessarily produce a written pledge, thereby leaving room for misunderstanding

Faith Covenant Sunday Appeals
   Extremely popular amongst evangelical communities, the Faith Covenant Sunday format seeks to produce a quantifiable financial commitment or pledge from every household, based upon an appeal to the strength of one's personal faith. This approach differs from most other financial appeals in that the pledge cards are collected during what is generally a highly motivational and emotionally charged worship service. Further, all that is recorded is the amount of money pledged, and the frequency with which it might be given. The desire to match people's understanding and love of the God with their commitment to provide a commensurate financial pledge is laudable, but if not administered extremely well,

can leave donors with the unfortunate but aptly described impression that "the church gets us on our knees to take our wallets."

Regrettably, Faith Covenant Sunday appeal programs tend to wildly overestimate financial giving prospects. Maybe this is because exuberance and group dynamics can lead people to "over promise;" maybe it is because people's names are not attached to the pledge cards; or maybe it is because commitments are made on the spot, without careful reflection and prayer. Whatever the reason, churches which lack several years' experience administering the program are ill-equipped to know how much to "discount" pledges as over against actual gifts received (creating a baseline), and as a result, can quickly find themselves in serious financial trouble. Moreover, the sense of "failure" churches can experience when they realize the significant gap between these two figures can be distressing and de-motivating, further alienating members from financial appeals and stewardship in general.

SOME FAITH COVENANT SUNDAY APPEAL MERITS:
- Can promote a healthy sense that stewardship is congruent with our faith life
- Can be quickly implemented with limited resources

SOME FAITH COVENANT SUNDAY APPEAL CONCERNS:
- Highly impersonal
- Enthusiastic group dynamics can lead to over-generous declarations
- Creates difficulty in following up with reminder letters and envelopes, as pledge cards generally omit individual contact information
- Unlikely to create contacts with "marginal members/adherents" and shut-ins
- Can create feelings of "coercion", "oppression" and "guilt" if not administered with a great deal of pastoral care and concern

Community-Based Approaches

Some churches opt for annual financial appeals that are community-based. These appeals are far more successful than such highly impersonal methods as the telephone canvass, or direct mail, but as we shall see presently, are less effective than personal appeals to individuals. Community-based approaches commonly take one of the following forms or names:

Cottage Meeting Appeal

This approach encourages every members to attend a presentation in the home of another member, who acts as "host" for the cottage meeting. Ordinarily, a team from the congregational stewardship committee makes a presentation to the group gathered at each cottage meeting, addressing the congregation's financial needs for the upcoming year. (Sometimes, but less often, the need for talented volunteers is addressed simultaneously.) These presentations tend to be fairly informal, relying upon photocopied handouts and poster charts, as opposed to overhead projection slides or computer-generated presentations. Members are generally asked to declare their financial commitment (pledge) for the upcoming year either at the end of the cottage meeting, or during a worship service the following Sunday.

SOME COTTAGE MEETING APPEAL MERITS:

- Respectful of limited resources, requiring only a few meetings
- Involves few people to organize and make presentations
- Ensures consistency in the funding message, as it is entrusted to only a few interpreters
- Provides an immediate forum in which to collect annual financial commitment declarations
- Cost-effective to the church in that dessert and coffee or wine and cheese are normally provided by the host

SOME COTTAGE MEETING APPEAL CONCERNS:

- Can require several homes for large churches since the size of homes limits the maximum number of participants
- Engages only a few members in the "leadership" of promoting stewardship
- Invests a feeling of "importance" and "responsibility" in a small group of members
- Calls for numerous meetings to be able to provide enough forums for every member to attend
- Causes difficulty in scheduling individual members to attend specific cottage meetings
- Necessitates either an intense number of meetings in a short period of time, or fewer meetings over a longer period of time: in either case, can overwhelm the liturgical and program focus of the congregation

Annual Congregational Dinner Appeal

Eliciting and encouraging the annual financial declaration of members through this method can create a highly sociable and enjoyable way of gathering the community for a shared purpose. The annual congregational dinner approach is invariably the "big event" of the year for such churches, should it not be, the likelihood of universal attendance is seriously compromised. As in the cottage meeting appeal, a small core of leaders from the congregational stewardship committee makes a presentation to the gathered members, outlining the financial projections and needs of the congregation for the coming year. However, these presentations are generally more professional, and high-tech, and supported by the distribution of an information packet for each household to take home and review. The solicitation of financial commitments (pledges) is seldom conducted during the dinner, and more often occurs during a special worship service the following day (annual congregational dinners often take place Saturday night).

SOME ANNUAL CONGREGATIONAL DINNER APPEAL MERITS:
- Requires only one evening to complete
- Requires few people to organize and make presentations
- Ensures a consistent message as it is invested in only a few people
- Provides an almost immediate forum in which to collect annual financial commitment declarations
- Can involve a number of committees including planning, cooking, room set-up, decoration, etc.
- Easy to promote—using the church bulletin, notice boards or a single congregation-wide mailing

SOME ANNUAL CONGREGATIONAL DINNER APPEAL CONCERNS:
- Can require off-site location if the church's hall is not adequate for the "big event"
- Whether prepared by members or provided by caterers, the cost of a meal enticing enough to encourage attendance can be prohibitive, sometimes overwhelmingly so in the first few years before it "catches on"
- Depends upon all households being available on the same evening
- Requires the production and distribution of attractive and information-rich materials for every household
- Can exclude shut-ins, and—if accessibility is a problem for the church—the physically challenged
- Is unlikely to pique the interest of less interested or marginally associated individuals
- Social atmosphere of event can undermine or overwhelm the importance of the topic
- Social setting may discourage tough questions or expressions of concern

Commitment Sunday Appeal

Sunday services draw the greatest number of individuals to the church on a regular basis. Implementing the congregation's financial appeal preceding, during, or after Sunday worship can help ensure that the maximum number of members receive the church's financial message in a timely manner. Like all the previously mentioned community-based financial appeal programs, the commitment Sunday appeal is generally associated with a financial commitment declaration (pledge) by which the church can measure its "success." Commitment Sunday appeals can vary from a strictly theological message to an unapologetic financial presentation, or a blend of both. In many cases, the special "draw" to such a service is a high-profile preacher, presenter, or even a denominational leader.

SOME COMMITMENT SUNDAY APPEAL MERITS:
- Requires only one Sunday to complete
- Is frequently associated with a high profile preacher, motivational speaker/presenter or denominational leader
- Promotes the concept of stewardship commitment as an intrinsic part of our lives as Christians
- Provides an immediate forum in which to collect annual financial commitment declarations
- Easy to promote—using the church bulletin, notice boards or a single membership mailing
- Requires almost no resources beyond announcements and a possible stipend for the guest preacher, speaker, presenter or denominational leader

SOME COMMITMENT SUNDAY APPEAL CONCERNS:
- Generally requires several "information" sessions prior to the commitment Sunday appeal
- Depends upon all households being available for a particular service

- In the context of a liturgical setting, the appeal can be easily viewed as coercive
- Disrupts the worship calendar or mediates the sacred nature of Sabbath observance
- Is unlikely to pique the interest of less interested or marginally associated individuals
- Communal atmosphere of worship service can have the unintended consequence of leading people to declare their financial commitment in a moment of exuberance, rather than as the result of prayerful consideration and reason
- The constraints of liturgical demeanor usually preclude the opportunity for questions or expressions of concern

Individual-Based Approaches

By far the most successful annual stewardship appeals enable the needs of the congregation as a whole to intersect with the personal understanding and commitment of individual members. Individual-based approaches give members and supporters the information and answers they need, and enough time to prayerfully consider their own resources and how best to render them in the service of God's Kingdom. An important feature of these appeals is that information is provided to members well in advance of a personal meeting. This allows members to reach their decisions prayerfully, thoughtfully, and reasonably, in the privacy of their own home. The meetings which follow are thus primarily an opportunity to have questions answered, and for those who act as "visitors" to receive a written financial declaration (pledge), thereby ensuring that the information and pledge cycle is completed. Some of traditional individual-based approaches include:

Personal Delivery Approach

This is the least personal of all the individual-based appeals. The system is very methodical. In preparation, the entire membership list is sorted into "teams," generally of no more than ten households each. The number of teams is thus dependent upon the size of the church or organization. The process begins with the "team leader" delivering the financial needs and appeal (generally in the form of written materials) to the second person on the team. After receiving and turning in the financial declaration (pledge) of this second person, the work of the team leader is finished. It is then the responsibility of the second team member to visit the third household on the team list, and so on, until every household on the team has not only been visited and made a financial declaration (pledge), but has visited another household to do the same. By having all teams begin their work at the same time, and assuming one visit per week, the church or ministry can expect to complete the personal delivery approach within a ten-week period.

SOME PERSONAL DELIVERY APPEAL MERITS:

- Encourages every family to take responsibility for the financial needs of the church or ministry
- Can create standing "teams" of people who can be used for many purposes, including prayer chains or other community-based initiatives
- Treats every household equally, embodying the Christian idea of community
- Completes an every household visitation in a fairly short period of time
- Relatively cost-effective
- Helps to verify and "clean up" the mailing list (addresses, phone numbers, etc.)
- Can be used to collect additional useful information, such as who needs pastoral care ministry
- Ensures that each household receives a visit (shut-ins are scheduled last so that their visit concludes each team's responsibility, and the house-bound are not required to make a visit)

SOME PERSONAL DELIVERY APPEAL CONCERNS:

- Assumes that each household is willing to visit another
- Invariably receives "uneven" responses, as some teams will be unable or unwilling to complete their expected visits
- Can be an impediment to members having their questions answered, since it is highly improbable that all members are uniformly knowledgeable about the needs, or equally capable of responding accurately and helpfully to questions and concerns
- Creates uncomfortable situations in which untrained volunteers can be viewed as "pressuring" or "coercing" their fellow members to make unusually large pledges out of a sense of embarrassment

Every Household Visitation

This is perhaps the best known financial appeal program. It has not only provided the most money for the church or ministry; when properly administered according to the values of passionate stewardship, it has the potential to transcend its mere financial benefits, and help to build a more cohesive and lively Christian community. This approach begins with an announcement that individual household visits will be taking place over a specified period. A corps of "visitors" are identified and educated about the financial needs, and taught how to discuss these needs in a pastorally sensitive manner within the context of the church's or ministry's overall sense of stewardship. Each of these visitors is then assigned ten (or fewer) households to visit. During these household visits, the visitor answers any questions their fellow members might have, and solicits an annual financial declaration (pledge). The strength of the every household visitation approach is that it seeks to arrange a private meeting between a trained and educated "visitor" in the familiar and comfortable surroundings of an individual's own home.

The principal failure in campaigns of this kind is the reluctance of the leadership to believe they can recruit enough volunteers to complete the program, and/or the failure actually to visit every household. Because of this fear or lack of faith, churches and other Christian ministries often follow the lead of secular fundraisers, and restrict their visits to those they believe will give the majority of money (thereby exacerbating the institutional welfare dynamic). This problem is almost always associated with a church or ministry that uses some system designed to "segment" or "target" members according to their perceived wealth, such that "advanced gift prospects," or "major gift prospects" are visited first. When this happens, the church or ministry usually expends all its time, talent and energy on a select and limited number of households. If the annual financial goal is met through the visits to this subset of the Christian community, volunteers inevitably lose their motivation to visit the rest, or feel no need to do so. As previously noted, this continues the counterproductive consequence of "investing" the responsibility for financial stewardship in a small number of households.

SOME EVERY HOUSEHOLD VISITATION APPEAL MERITS:
- Engages every individual and household in taking responsibility for the financial needs of the church or ministry
- Can create standing "teams" of people who can be used for many purposes, including prayer chains or other community-based initiatives
- When there is no segmentation into "target" groups, it treats every household as equals, promoting the Christian idea of community
- Completes an every-household visitation in a fairly short period of time
- Relatively cost-effective

- Provides a forum for professionalized teaching of stewardship and basic pastoral care practices/concerns to a corps of volunteers for ministry
- Helps to verify and "clean up" the database
- Confidential context of a home visit creates the most desirable environment for members to ask questions and receive information
- Can be used to collect additional useful information, such as who is in need of pastoral care
- Ensures that each household receives a visit
- When organized properly, the conduct of the visits helps to connect members who may not know each other very well (i.e. builds and strengthens personal relationships)

SOME EVERY HOUSEHOLD VISITATION APPEAL CONCERNS:
- Requires a corps of volunteers for stewardship ministry who will actually complete the ministry they take on as "visitors"
- Generally needs the assistance of an experienced outside consultant to help shape the appeal program, train "visitors," and coordinate the significant amount of volunteer ministry and information during the effort
- Requires a sizable investment of time, talent and treasure to administer the program properly (although the return rate makes this appeal the most financially "successful")
- Requires volunteers who are mature and pastorally sensitive, and may thus limit the number of people suitable for this ministry

All the aforementioned programs have features to commend them, although some certainly more than others. It is important to remember that no two churches or ministries are alike, and therefore, there is no "one size fits all" plan which can be applied in cookie-cutter fashion to our various communities. My own experience is that each model requires different talents, and all require the requisite experience to anticipate those inherent pitfalls which would announce themselves in an unpracticed hand, as well as to handle the foibles and sensitivities of the eclectic community of persons who are the Body of Christ. While the church or ministry can continue to rely upon stewardship consultants to offer unbiased and extra-community experience and wisdom, a proper and desirable goal, if we are to thrive in the future, is for the church or ministry to provide such counsel using internal resources.

The level of skill and knowledge required to provide excellence in stewardship ministry is likely more than can be developed within individual churches or ministries. A good stewardship leader almost certainly has experience of multiple churches, and preferably of several denominations. If we are to liberate ourselves from the need to hire outside consultants—and most especially consultants who employ secular fundraising practices "dressed up" for churches—we shall need to convince the church and ministry leadership to create an environment in which skilled stewardship leaders can be made *meaningfully* available at the local church, ministry or community level.

Annual financial campaigns, though only one part of the triune complex of time, talent, and treasure, are so visibly a feature of congregational life that we can only hope to recover a thoroughly Christian model of stewardship if we can assist churches and other Christian ministries to embrace thoroughly Christian principles in running them.

Chapter XIV
Special Financial and Capital Campaigns

Inevitably the time comes when any church or faith-based charity must raise an extraordinary amount of money in a time-limited manner. When this is done to establish or perpetuate a given ministry or program, we generally call such efforts "Special Financial Campaigns"—"special" because they are administered to raise funds over and above the regular collection upon which the church or ministry relies, and "financial" because the traditional goal of such campaigns has been to raise money—and generally only money.

"Capital Campaigns" differ only in that the financial proceeds are generally restricted to capital needs, as for example, the construction of a Christian school, church, or hall; or the maintenance and improvement of existing physical structures. Like Special Financial Campaigns, Capital Campaigns have usually been focused solely on money. This is problematic, however, since—as has been made clear—money should never be the only goal, considering that we can engage in real and passionate stewardship in the same time-limited period with equal, if not superior, financial results. Campaigns can be so much more than mere financial exercises to perpetuate our organizational existence. They should, can, and must be recovered as opportunities for engaging the faithful in the life of stewardship.

Most churches and organizations where I have worked have a collective memory of some previous campaign (whether recent or long past). During our preliminary discussions, I invariably receive more instructions about what people *don't* want than what they *do*. I suggest that this stems less from a clear sense of vision respecting stewardship and fundraising than from negative prior experiences, and similar tales of woe from friends. This is the consequence of abandoning our own first principles. Hence, before treating the actual elements of campaign administration, it behooves us to reiterate our fundamental priorities for Christian stewardship. Throughout this chapter, for the purposes of illustration, we shall treat the campaign as a congregational activity; it should be noted, however, that the issues raised apply similarly to other faith-based organizations.

It is difficult to write about special financial and capital campaigns without falling into the trap of writing a "how to" manual or a "step by step" guide. However, just as the discussion of good stewardship can be grounded in certain fundamental principles, so can our consideration of special campaigns. For the most part, our decision-making needs to be guided by three basic concerns:

1. Is what we are doing consistent with our stated beliefs, and the values of the church?
2. How does any given task or action further the individual member's stewardship journey?
3. Does the campaign encourage gifts in a manner that preserves the dignity of the Body of Christ and respects the dignity of Christians asked to contribute their time, talent and treasure?

These three principles cannot be done justice by the "cookie-cutter" templates for fundraising usually presented to the church, as though they were options on a menu. Campaigns must be planned, administered and grounded in the particular needs of each congregation, carefully cognizant of its size, socio-economic circumstances and history, and tailored specifically to the progress of the members in their stewardship journey.

Vision – Planning for the Future

Most churches undertake a special financial or capital campaign to meet a recognized financial need. It is noteworthy and troubling that the need for money, rather than forward planning, is what prompts most such campaigns. There is some kind of crisis: revenues are falling short of expenditures, the roof is leaking with the first spring rain, the boiler has quit in the midst of winter, or the foundation has cracked unexpectedly after decades of service. Almost without thinking, the congregation slips into reactivity: *Quick! We need money.* How different from the kind of proactive thinking whereby needs are projected well in advance, so that campaigns need not be administered in the context of impending or actual crisis.

Granted, constant social and economic shifts may require a certain flexibility and reactivity in our program and outreach ministries—at times even necessitating capital projects, including church planting and expansion. However, this should not be the case with respect to general capital and maintenance planning. Recognizing this dynamic is key to understanding how ongoing stewardship, which always entails good planning, will not only reduce the frequency with which campaigns are necessary, but what, how, and whose, time and talent will be made available to carry out such campaigns.

Needs Assessment

Before beginning a campaign a congregation should have a basic understanding not only of the financial needs they are facing, but why providing the money to satisfy these needs will make a difference in the lives of believers and, more importantly, of those who rely upon the church for its ministries and witness. After all, people are seldom motivated to give just because the church needs money. Rather, they will give generously of their time, talent and treasure when they understand how their gift will make a difference, and most especially how their gift is a response to the call of the Holy Spirit to witness to the loving care of Christ for all. This is not mere pious rhetoric, but rather a prophetic call to a richer view of stewardship, and a solemn refusal to limit it to simple fundraising.

Needs assessment is thus about more than a cost-analysis of physical needs. It is also about people. That is, it includes an evaluation of what (and who) is needed to conduct a successful campaign in a manner which simultaneously respects the needs of the people involved. Even where socio-economic factors would indicate that a significant amount of money is available to the congregation, should volunteers for stewardship ministry, committee work, and campaign volunteers not be forthcoming, the money will remain uncommitted, uncollected, and unemployed in the service of Christ. A particular challenge for many communities is the secretarial component of campaign administration and follow-up. Campaigns are administratively intensive, and may require more time (and sometimes more skill or resources) than the average congregational secretary has to give. How will the church address this need? Similarly, because of the demands on available time in many of today's households, it must be determined not only who will volunteer, but when, under what conditions, and with what support, if they are to successfully and happily undertake the ministry of stewardship and fundraising in the congregation. Therefore, determining the amount of money needed must be matched with a determination of how many people, with what needs, might give of their time and talent to help the church achieve its financial goals.

The Development Study

Generally, in preparing for congregational campaigns, some sort of "feasibility study" has been conducted to help the congregation understand how much money it might raise. Note how, from the very beginning, the term "feasibility" restricts the goal of these studies and campaigns to money, not stewardship.

Feasibility connotes financial success, and leaves aside such questions as *How?* and *Why?* As a rule, such studies are limited to a series of questions that seek to identify the amount of money people might give, and what expectation of recognition or control they expect to have in connection with their "gift." By reducing our interest in people to how much they might give, fundraising feasibility studies have objectified members and adherents—essentially treating them as wallets—rather than according them the dignity which belongs to them by virtue of their membership in the Body of Christ, and treating them as persons who will themselves make an offering for the sake of the dignity of those they now know to be in need.

The development study is much different. The very term "development" helps members approach the study more holistically, and to avoid the concern and apprehension which naturally attach to an appraisal of "feasibility." Development studies do assess financial potential. However, they are also, and equally, an opportunity for the church to ask about members' experience of the many ministries the congregation undertakes (both from a volunteer and recipient perspective), and to understand how people's background might impact on such issues as their spiritual, theological and religious development, why they volunteer for ministry, when they are available to volunteer, and what talents they might have and be willing to contribute.

The assessment of these issues is critical to building a stewardship-driven campaign. Without understanding where people have been, how they perceive the church, where they want to go, and what they are willing to do to reach their individual and shared goals, the congregation is deprived of the ability to design a campaign that responds to, creates or redirects enthusiasm for anything other than financial needs. For this reason the development study may be more critical to the campaign's success than anything else. It is thus always helpful for someone knowledgeable about stewardship and the campaign to assist in designing the study. Experience also shows that the value of such studies is much enhanced by the use of a trusted and independent individual who can receive information confidentially, and who is able to communicate his or her findings to the congregation in an effective and non-threatening manner for corrective action and/or implementation.

The Role and Benefit of Consultants

For this reason, I believe that any church development process should include the assistance of someone who regularly teaches and leads stewardship. It is not necessary to retain a fundraiser *per se*. What is required is someone from outside the congregation who can serve as an impartial guide in developing and assessing process, and in recruiting, training, and managing volunteers. Unfortunately, few churches, have someone on staff that is trained, or if trained, who is in a position to serve as independent and impartial counsel. More than this, as noted earlier, such "experts" in stewardship are unlikely to have the available time for the intensive and ongoing involvement a campaign requires.

The willingness of a congregation to invite an "outsider" into their process can be critical to the overall success of a campaign. While churches may begin by seeking the knowledge and experience a stewardship consultant can bring, they often discover that their real need is the consultant's ability to teach and demonstrate leadership without taking control, assuming authority, or taking responsibility for the campaign. The administration, authority and responsibility for campaigns must reside in the church's leadership, and not be relinquished to "others" who are, after all, not long-term stakeholders in the congregation. Not only will this encourage members to embrace stewardship as their own responsibility, but it will help to develop internal leaders and expertise which will remain in the congregation even after the consultant leaves.

Consultants from a ministry-base external to the congregation have the unique advantage of not being invested in past decisions, mistakes, problems or points of view within the congregation. Being "unblemished" by the past allows external consultants to act, speak—and listen—freely, and enables them to establish their integrity and authority through the exercise of their stewardship ministry in the congregation. The appropriate consultant can and should be someone with the pastoral sensitivity and stewardship experience to be a trusted recipient of the kind of private information that informs the congregation's decision-making about the generous giving of their time, talent and treasure.

For the church leader, this can be a challenging exercise in humility. The truth is that the opinions of an "outside" expert are frequently held in higher regard than those of the pastor or church leadership. It is a failing of human nature that we are prepared to hear from others the very same thing which falls upon deaf ears when told us by our families and neighbors. The Hebrew Scriptures show that Israel frequently persecuted the prophets, and Jesus himself taught that no prophet is accepted in his own land. The need to continue to live peaceably in a community where hard truths must sometimes be spoken, means that church leaders and pastors are sometimes hampered in their ability to point out troubled areas and issues in need of improvement. The consultant can help the congregation successfully navigate those issues which might otherwise be avoided for fear of conflict.

Choosing a Consultant

Because most fundraisers focus their energy and hone their techniques in the more financially lucrative area of secular fundraising, the local church is frequently and uncritically subjected to the same secular assumptions and methods when it invites such fundraisers to work with it. It is thus important to ensure that any consultant retained to assist the congregation be a person of faith, and knowledgeably adept with respect to congregational dynamics, pastoral issues, and interpersonal relationships.

The selection of a consultant need not be a source of anxiety if proper scrutiny is exercised. Many churches, for example, have mistakenly focused their attention on the reputation and track record of the firm being considered, rather than on the consultant that firm would assign. A firm can offer little more than clerical support and general procedures for their fundraisers to employ. In the end, it is the individual with whom you will work that matters. It is thus critical to meet, interview, and scrutinize the individual on-site consultant(s) before entering any contractual agreement. It is this person's experience, track record, pastoral sensitivity, and personal rapport with the congregational leadership that will truly make the difference for the church. An unseasoned and/or inexperienced consultant from even the best of firms must rely upon superiors to help unravel problems that their inexperience keeps them from anticipating and preventing, or identifying and solving. Even more than their knowledge base, it is the ability to foresee and avoid conflict and problems that makes a consultant beneficial to the congregation.

Planning the Campaign

Christian book stores and libraries are full of books which set forth various methods of administering campaigns. Church leaders can learn much from most of these books. However, the assumption that any given campaign plan will serve all churches equally well defies reason. Congregations are as unique as the people who comprise them: each community presents a different constellation of socio-economic backgrounds, confessional development, prior congregational experiences, and individual understandings not only of stewardship but of the issues driving the current need to conduct a campaign. Generally helpful though the literature on fundraising, campaigns, and stewardship may be, no book or manual on its own can provide an approach that respects the particularities of an individual congregation.

The development study is therefore critical in eliciting the information necessary to design a successful, stewardship-based campaign. If the appropriate information is not collected in the development study, the campaign plan will be experienced as little more than a generic method superimposed on a generic "donor base." This is what we mean by a "process-driven" approach. The church, however, has a higher calling, which is to structure its work in a way that attends to the needs of people. The development study should therefore touch not only on matters about which the congregation would like particular feedback (e.g. program or ministry satisfaction, ideas about space utilization), but at a minimum:

- What problems or conflicts exist in the congregation that might detract from a campaign?
- What does the congregation do well that can be communicated effectively?
- What impact will the congregation's history of stewardship and, in particular, past campaign experiences have on the proposed campaign? What issues need correction during the campaign?
- How does the congregation understand stewardship values, and particular program or project needs? What specific education must take place to satisfy members' need for accurate, sensible and stewardship-driven information?
- Whom will the congregation embrace as campaign chairs and/or co-chairs? (Encouraging members to select the chairs is critical, whereas historically the chairs were appointed, and the congregation asked to accept them.)
- What kind of leadership, division of responsibilities, and accountability does the congregation seek in the administration of the campaign?

- What kind of campaign structure will members respond to best?
- What particular training and skills will campaign volunteers need in order to confidently carry out their ministry?
- Who will volunteer, and in what circumstances will they volunteer (e.g. time commitment required, support mechanisms, materials, etc.)?
- How many members will volunteer to work on the campaign? (This has a significant impact on how the campaign is organized and designed.)
- How much money might be donated and with what expectations (i.e. donor recognition, project oversight, financial accountability, and other particular needs or demands being met)?
- What kind of campaign plan would encourage the greatest number of members to donate? (Campaign design and organization can help encourage the broadest participation possible, which correlates directly with "ownership" of the campaign, its goals and responsibilities.)
- When should the campaign be conducted?
- What confidential information might be received by the study director(s) that might not otherwise be shared with the pastor and leadership of the congregation?

This is not an exhaustive list, but it does identify basic information critical to the design of a healthy and successful campaign. Should this information be unsolicited, ignored, or overlooked, churches will find themselves squeezed into a boiler-plate campaign plan, as opposed to embracing a campaign tailored to meet their evolving needs and unique character. No two churches are identical. Demographics and economic characteristics will vary, as will the views of the pastors and leadership on stewardship and congregational development. Churches are at different stages of congregational development, and different places in their communal faith journey. Needs and goals differ, too. For this reason a campaign plan which fails to take account of the congregation's peculiarities and uniqueness will fail likewise to seize the opportunity to nurture the spiritual, religious, and theological development of individual stewards. It will be precisely the kind of "money only" campaign that undercuts genuine stewardship.

Recruiting Volunteers for Stewardship Ministry

In recruiting volunteers for ministry it is important to be cognizant of the dynamics of leadership and interpersonal relationships. To "let our yes be yes" (Jas 5:12), we need to rethink the conventional wisdom about sending "the right person to ask." When a pastor or other church leader asks a member to volunteer, this may create an essentially manipulative power dynamic in which the member feels uncomfortable saying no. He or she may not want to disappoint the pastor, or appear to be uncommitted to the church. Whether the pressure is real or imagined, it is not uncommon for members in this situation to say yes, but half-heartedly. This is no place from which to embark upon a ministry which carries a volunteer deep into the journey of stewardship. It is thus essential to give members the information they need to come to an informed and prayerful decision about their involvement in the congregation's stewardship ministry. Yes needs to mean yes; and it is all right to say no.

The first step in recruiting volunteers for any stewardship effort is to ensure that stewardship, and not mere fundraising, is at the heart of the ministry. For this reason it is extremely useful for potential volunteers to receive a brief vision statement about the goals of the campaign, their own role, and an accurate description of the specific duties and demands that will be made of them. This written outline is analogous to the position description one would expect when considering a job. The only difference is the inclusion of the vision statement, which places the volunteer's proposed role within the total context of ministry and the congregation. Churches which dispense with such a volunteer ministry description often find that members are either unwilling to commit because of their unaddressed concerns about the demands to be made of them; or members who do volunteer may later have regrets when their duties and responsibilities exceed their understanding of what was expected.

Moreover, people who volunteer without understanding what will be expected of them commonly find their ministry laborious, and as a result, may avoid doing what they agreed to do, thereby creating disappointment on the part of both the volunteer, and campaign leaders. There is no excuse for allowing poor management to alienate a member from the church he or she loves. Good stewardship entails caring for the resources entrusted to us—and this includes the gift of people's time and talents. Taking the time to engage in expectation management is a powerful way of demonstrating our care for people who give so generously of themselves.

The way campaign volunteers are recruited can have a long-term impact on the church's ability to engage members for future volunteer ministries, whether to teach Sunday school, help with a literacy program, or visit the sick. The campaign presents an opportunity to demonstrate that the congregation is committed to mutual stewardship, in which the church cares for volunteers, and volunteers care for the church. It can also be an opportunity to recover these values if members have had poor volunteer experience in the past.

There are a number of basic rules for volunteer management. Chief among these is the overarching obligation to ensure that the church is a good steward of its own stewards. It is said that in 258 C.E. when St. Laurence the Martyr was made to hand over the riches of the local church to the state authority, he went out and gathered the poor, the elderly, and the dispossessed; and setting them before the magistrate, said, "Here are the treasures of the church." Laurence understood, as we must, that it is above all people who are our greatest gift and resource.

At the heart of any volunteer's first gift is time. Unfortunately, time is the most abused of all of our resources. How often are members told that a meeting will start and end at a specific time, only to have the meeting start late and end even later, forcing them to neglect other responsibilities? Considering that most congregational meetings take place in the evening, the church needs to remember that most participants have already made a sacrifice of precious time with their families in order even to be present. Beginning meetings on time, ending on time, and coming fully prepared to each meeting is the first principle of demonstrating good stewardship of the gift of time.

The recognition of individual members' talents is also cause for reflection. Too often, the campaign plan is "struck in stone" before taking account of the gifts already resident within the congregation. The result is that we end up matching members to pre-defined ministries, without prior regard for their particular talents or gifts. A good campaign plan will draw on the talents and gifts of as many members as possible, be they great or small. It is important, even if inconvenient and demanding, to ensure, for example, that artists find an artistic outlet within the campaign, that accountants be given an opportunity to assist in its financial administration, and that particular care is taken to find appropriate tasks for those who are infirm, or who might otherwise be sidelined. (Preparing mailings could be one such task.) Engaging as many people as possible in the campaign, in whatever capacity, will go a long way to helping members take personal ownership of the communal values undergirding the campaign. To make the campaign team as large as possible runs counter to most secular campaign models where efficiency, return on investment, and streamlining are the order of the day. The church, however, values time, talent *and* treasure in equal measure. Hence, every effort must be made to receive the gift that members can and want to give, according to both their means and their faith. As we have stated elsewhere, the gift of time and talent is often the best indication of people's willingness to give of their treasure, too. Campaigns which don't encourage the involvement of as many members as possible tend to grossly under-achieve their financial potential.

Conducting the Campaign

Promoting awareness of the campaign is an opportunity for every church committee to get involved, each within the parameters of its own mandate. The congregational outreach committee can make posters describing how the campaign will assist the ministry of outreach; the welcoming committee can explain the campaign's goals and objectives to newer members; the building committee can make a presentation about how the facilities will be differently used, or improved to accommodate the ministries and programs that underlie the need for the campaign; the finance committee can make itself available after services to explain the technical aspects of campaign financing; the hospitality committee can prepare food and refreshments for campaign volunteer training sessions; and the kick-off reception and worship/liturgy committees can help plan the liturgy to launch the campaign. Every church committee should be represented and involved in the planning, support, and administration of the campaign at all critical points.

Launching the campaign in the context of worship helps people understand that the campaign is about more than money, and that stewardship is itself a ministry within the church. The ancient custom of commissioning people for ministry can be an excellent way to kick off a campaign. By calling forth the campaign volunteers and commissioning them for their ministry, the church puts stewardship in its proper context, and also encourages members to locate their personal stewardship journey in the larger framework of their vocation to follow Christ.

The commissioning of campaign volunteers can be as simple as this:

Pastor   Over the past few years our congregation has been engaged in a process of discernment about our ministry, our facilities and our future. The outcome of that process was the recognition that this congregation's future depends upon our ability to support worship and ministry by *[repairing our building, providing more multi-purpose space and creating better physical accessibility for all God's people]*.

With the fruits of our vision supported by a long period of investigation and planning, we are now within sight of fulfilling our goals. To do this we have decided to conduct a capital campaign to raise the money to help make our ministry happen. After much prayer and consideration we have called this campaign *["Forward in Faith"]*, to clearly describe our fervent Christian hope and belief that we can *[continue to give witness to our ministry for years to come]*.

We now commission our campaign visitors who will undertake their ministry to visit each household in the congregation, encouraging personal financial support for the campaign to build up our church facilities, in order that our physical facilities might meet our ministry and outreach needs.

Will the capital campaign visitors please come forward and be recognized?

Visitors come forward to the front of the church.

Pastor   You have undertaken an important ministry in this congregation. Will you promise to do all that you can to

encourage and invite the people of our faith community to participate more fully in the life of our congregation?
Visitors Yes, I will.

Pastor   Will you carry out your ministry in keeping with the spirit and guidance of the Holy Spirit and the Gospels?
Visitors Yes, I will.

Pastor   Will you encourage and support each other in your ministry of visiting?
Visitors Yes, I will.

Pastor   Will you pray for God's blessing on this congregation, and upon your ministry in supporting our church, serving Christ and God's Kingdom?
Visitors Yes, I will.

Pastor   My fellow members, please stand for your responses.

All stand.

Pastor   Do you, the congregation of *[the Christian Church of _____]* promise to receive our campaign visitors in the spirit of friendship and community as they carry out their ministry?
People   Yes, we will.

Pastor   Will you consider supporting this congregation so that we can continue our commitment to Christian ministry and outreach?
People   Yes, we will.

Pastor   Will you promise to pray for those who have undertaken the ministry of campaign visitor so that they might be strengthened and supported in the conduct of their ministry to God's People?

People   Yes, we will.

Pastor   Will you consider the gifts that the Father has bestowed upon you throughout your lives, pray for the commitment shown by Jesus, and for the loving guidance of the Holy Spirit, that you might be endowed with the spirit of Christian generosity, as you consider your role as a steward of Christ's Church?

People   Yes, we will.

Pastor turns to face the campaign visitors.

Pastor   Having given your promises to build up God's Church through your ministry as campaign visitors, I commission you and bless you in the name of the Father, and of the Son, and of the Holy Spirit.

People   Amen.

Pastor   Be assured of my prayers and support as you undertake this important mission.

Let us pray.

Heavenly Father, bless these campaign visitors, and guide them in your ways as they seek to build up your Church on earth. Christ Jesus, give them the courage, wisdom and strength to share in your work, that we might all rejoice in this season of renewal. Holy Spirit, renew us all and remember your people who seek to glorify your Holy Name, through Christ Jesus, our Savior, Redeemer, and Lord of all.

People   Amen.

The public commissioning of visitors for their ministry serves to remind all members that it is from the depths of their vocation as stewards that they will be asked to make a gift to the campaign. Only when the church truly grounds its requests for assistance in the vocation of Christian stewardship, will we elicit generous gifts to God, as opposed to monetary contributions to an organization. When people have embraced a theology of abundance, and set out on the path of passionate stewardship, they will give freely and generously.

One of the worst errors a congregation can make is to follow the secular practice of segmenting households for the purposes of gift or pledge solicitation in accordance with perceived socio-economic status or ability to give. This approach can be extremely harmful to the congregation's sense of *communitas,* since members are led to believe that their value to the community is contingent not on generosity, but upon their social standing and ability to bankroll the organization.

Campaigns need not follow the secular pattern of reaching 50% of the campaign's goal before the campaign is even made public. This strategy virtually requires that members of greater financial standing be visited first, in order that a few large gifts be secured. This commences the cycle of segmentation. There is no self-evident or compelling reason to administer campaigns in this way. On the contrary, there is great dignity in visiting all members at the same time, inviting both rich and poor, weak and powerful equally into the congregation's life, and receiving their gifts on the same "holy ground," as God intended. The church can give the lie to the assumption that wealth drives charitable giving, and return instead to our ancient conviction that stewardship is driven by gratitude, witnessed by generosity and perfected by grace. This can be visualized in the following diagram:[54]

Expectation Management

In addition to keeping the campaign grounded in stewardship, leaders must pay careful attention to expectations. Members will inevitably import a kaleidoscope of previous campaign experiences, and attitudes towards stewardship, into their unspoken assumptions and expectations regarding any proposed campaign. Hence, it is important clearly to define the campaign's goals and objectives, and equally, to establish timelines and benchmarks for various campaign activities. Failure to do so may allow anxiety or concerns arising from previous experience (or no experience) to intrude upon the current campaign.

Managing expectations needs to begin at the planning stage. Leaders must not only understand what is expected of them, but when and how. Volunteers, too, are entitled to, and respond best to, clear expectations and objectives. Likewise, the congregation as a

---

[54] This graphic was developed by the Episcopal Diocese of Albany, and is used with permission.

whole needs to be kept "in the loop." Naturally, each of these constituencies will have different needs, depending upon the intensity of their involvement in the total campaign plan. For instance, a campaign chair will have to be far more informed about timelines for volunteer recruitment, and such benchmarks as printing deadlines, than the small group who will be asked to manage the celebratory party at the end of the campaign. Information needs to be delivered with the specific needs of the recipient in mind.

Therefore, not only what information is disseminated, but how it is disseminated, is important. Churches that publish a complete timeline, including preparatory meetings and deadlines which concern only a few people, risk having people believe that the campaign is interminable. Moreover, minute detail, widely distributed, invites minute criticism, widely offered—despite an ignorance of how various details may fit together. This must always, however, be balanced against the need for transparency, and access to information. Generally speaking, it is better to have a complete campaign plan available for inspection in the church's office, and someone appointed to brief inquisitive members, than to deluge members with far too much information in the misguided attempt to keep everyone fully informed.

Being cognizant of time, attention spans, and perception is also essential in the management of expectations. Members who feel that the campaign is dragging on are bound to have unnecessary anxiety about why it is taking so long to reach the financial goal. They may also become concerned that the campaign is overshadowing other important aspects of congregational life, such as liturgy, prayer, outreach, or other critical ministries and programs. The more that leadership communicates with the members, the better. One way of doing this is to prepare the congregation and its committees for the coming campaign at least a year in advance. This kind of long-term planning will help committees avoid the conflicts that inevitably occur when "suddenly" a major initiative must be pared back or put aside in order to accommodate the integration of a campaign into their work and ministry.

Follow-Up

A common failing of many campaigns, secular and faith-based, is inattention to follow-up once the campaign pledge phase is finished. Too often, we expend disproportionate energy in preparation for the pledge phase, only to fall short on the reception and administration of pledges throughout the collection period. Every church can expect some "fall off" in pledge redemption, but such circumstances should be limited to death, and departure, not dissatisfaction, or lack of diligence on the part of the congregation. The hallmark of a good campaign is not just the amount of money raised—although this is the easiest objective measure of a campaign's success—but, more importantly, the satisfaction members have first in making their pledge, and subsequently (absent any unforeseen personal difficulties) in fulfilling it.

Campaigns that are not rooted in an appeal to members' sense of stewardship become mere financial undertakings to support the institution. This dynamic can have dire consequences for pledge redemption, as people are more apt to let financial pledges go unredeemed when dissatisfaction with the campaign, congregation or church leadership outweighs their motivation for pledging or giving in the first place. Stewards, on the other hand, understand that gifts are made according to our faith, in appreciation for the bounty that God has bestowed upon us, and consequently, are not predisposed to allowing temporal conflicts to interfere with their desire to follow through on their freely given sacrifice of time, talent or treasure.

Taking the pledge redemption period seriously, planning the work and working the plan, is an integral part of every campaign, and should receive as much attention as any other phase of the campaign. Pledge redemption is not the only reason to ensure that this is so. The entire pledge period gives the church an opportunity to communicate the achievement of its goals, and monitor its progress in using donors' gifts to support of mission, ministry, bricks and mortar. People are thus encouraged to continue to value the objectives and goals which first necessitated the campaign. Pledge redemption isn't just about collecting money: it also provides an opportunity for understanding. Making frequent contact with members (at least every 6 months) is thus greatly preferable to providing redemption envelopes annually. Reaching the goal without then collecting the money is an exercise in futility, and is one of the areas in critical need of improvement in most church campaigns. Not least, pledge redemption invites and requires pastoral attentiveness, since an unredeemed pledge, so far from signifying a change in financial circumstances, may well be a first indication of spiritual crisis.

The more members see that they are valued not for their wealth, but for their inherent worth and dignity as human beings and members of the Christian family, the happier and more receptive they will be to the church's financial needs. The better people understand how their money supports the mission and ministry of the church, the more highly they will value the need to redeem their pledges, thereby reinforcing the cycle of grace begetting gratitude begetting generosity.

Chapter XV
Promoting Stewardship as a Life Choice –
Planned Giving and Legacies of Faith

One mark of good stewardship is that it comprises a lifelong attitude or posture towards the gifts that come into our hand. That is, the passionate steward never ceases to open his or her hand in service of the needs God continues to reveal to us. This is entirely different from the kind of fundraising or volunteer drive which gets rustled up as the urgent response to a problem which, truth be told, has been trying to announce itself for years. Good stewardship is not a response to crisis; it is not a crisis-management program: it is the Christian's way of life. This is, in part, what we mean by describing stewardship as "vocational." Only thus can we function without lurching from one calamity to another, constrained to seek quick fixes, and forced to rely upon the counsel of fundraising experts who are unable either to identify or embrace the unique and sanctifying nature of Christian stewardship.

Because good stewardship is unremitting, there will be, through the recovery of vocational stewardship, less need for the church to remedy the consequences of our past history of poor stewardship. Passionate stewardship promises a greater ability to tend to the present, and to provide for the future as we continue on our pilgrim way, responding more fully and appropriately to our understanding of God's call.

A particularly compelling example of the need for attentiveness to stewardly principles is the movement of the baby boom generation into old age. As can be clearly seen from the following chart, the "elderly" (aged 65 and over) are becoming an increasingly large percentage of the American population. In 1997, one in eight Americans was elderly. By the year 2030, the figure will be more like one in five.[55]

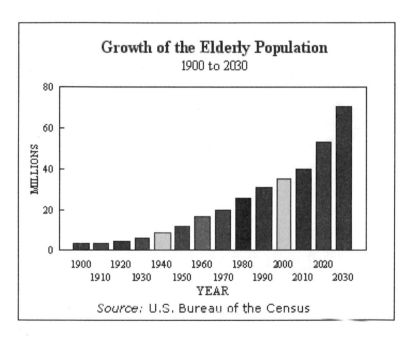

The situation is no different in Canada where, if anything, the trend is accelerated. The shift from the elderly being 13% of the population to an expected 21% of the population in the next generation will have major policy implications for society in general, and for the Christian community in particular. Indeed,

---

[55] Rachel Shapiro, "The Demographics of Aging in America," (U.S. Bureau of the Census: Population Resource Center, 1997).

given that the average age of members in historic, mainline churches exceeds that of society at large, these churches should brace themselves for more predominantly "gray haired" congregations over the next twenty years. Next to the demands of litigation being faced by some Christian denominations, meeting the needs of an aging congregation is arguably the most crucial and costly challenge facing churches today. It is in our best interest, therefore, to determine as fully as possible the impact this trend will have on the near term future of congregations, and on stewardship.

I suggest that we begin addressing these challenges at the level of gifts of time and talent. Traditionally, "volunteerism" has been closely tied to age. As people reached their retirement years and became "empty nesters," they had more time to devote to their leisure and charitable interests. Churches were the principal beneficiary, and these retirees, in turn, provided the bulk of the churches' volunteer time. However, during the past decade, there has been a decline of volunteerism amongst the baby-boom generation. People are busy, and baby boomers have learned that everything from sushi to snow shoveling can be had for a price. Consequently this is a generation which has tended to part with its money more readily than its time and talent. This has given rise to a growing concern that volunteerism is becoming an archaic value. Secular models of fundraising have only exacerbated this trend, by characterizing the donation of money as the most important sign of one's commitment to the congregation.

As we have already seen, however, the investment of one's time in the congregation is an important aspect of stewardship, not only because "hands-on" involvement deepens one's commitment to the Christian agenda, but also because it is closely correlated with a willingness to be generous with one's material resources. We also know (cf. p. 45) that people are much more likely to give of their time and talent if asked. It is essential for good stewardship, and for the future of the churches, therefore, that we address the issue of generosity with one's time as a matter of priority. We need to teach the offering of time, and we need to invite it.

But it isn't just as simple as that. The time and talent we are asking for belongs to people with creaky bones. Without question, an aging congregation is going to have to reconsider its physical facilities. Nor can full accessibility be limited to accommodating those confined to wheelchairs, or using walkers and other assistive devices, or whose mobility is compromised by bad knees, hip replacements, or poor stamina. Full accessibility includes making the church an open space for people with impaired vision or hearing, too. Given that the liturgy is so highly visual and aural, we can scarcely claim to be an accessible—let alone inclusive—community if people can't hear, or see, what is going on. It is imperative that our physical facilities are not themselves an impediment to the full participation of the People of God in the worship life of the church. Only thus will we be able to continue to engage in the mystery that is our faith.

This said, the requirement to improve accessibility in churches portends huge capital needs for older facilities. The cost of installing wheelchair ramps or elevators, and/or removing other physical barriers, as well as reconfiguring seating and sightlines, supplying large print hymn books, and providing or rehabilitating public address systems and other hearing assistance devices will be tremendous.

These needs are not confined to the worship space. Church basements and fellowship halls, which have normally been the social and program center of faith communities, also need attention. The greatest impediment to participation in the coffee hour, Bible study and other social, educational or volunteer ministry activities may be the number of stairs to be negotiated just to get there. As an ever-growing proportion of the Christian community faces the physical challenges of aging, physical barriers may present the greatest obstacle to their continued participation in, and commitment to, an inclusive and interactive community of faith.

These problems are already making themselves felt. Good sense dictates that we, the congregations, reflect proactively, *before* we find ourselves in a state of crisis, and needing to raise money without having given due consideration to either the need, or the best way forward. This will involve clearly identifying the problem, considering and settling upon a solution, and implementing the chosen alternative (cf. the diagram on p. 126). See how, just as described in the "Scenario" in Chapter XII, the recognition of a shared problem provides an opportunity to engage an entire community in the process of stewardship. By first taking the time to consider the impact of this demographic shift, and then drawing upon the talents of members to discover remedies for the problem (e.g. installing elevators, lifts, better sound systems, etc.), the church can position itself to solve its problems before they have a deleterious impact on attendance, volunteer ministry and community life. The time and talent that are devoted to these problems today will no doubt lay the groundwork for the offering of treasure required to implement a solution tomorrow. In this way, undertaking a critical assessment of our church buildings is not only a good starting point for proper strategic planning; it belongs to good stewardship itself.

Creating a Legacy of Faith

Just as the institutional church may undertake stewardship renewal by carefully identifying those problems which challenge its ability to fulfill its mission, and proposing solutions which will enable it to move forward, so may individual Christians embrace this kind of forward thinking and future planning in their own stewardship journey. If the congregation as a whole is ill-advised to limit stewardship to reactive programs of high focus or intensity, such as crisis-oriented campaigns, or even annual pledge appeals, then the individual member, too, must be encouraged to think in the long term, for the sake of the future. Stewardship needs to be freed from the limitations of spontaneity and annual giving, and allowed to flourish as a life-long and longer-than-life habit.

This invites a consideration of planned giving, or what may more aptly be called a "legacy of faith."

The fact that the baby boom generation is now reaching old age means that over the next two decades, both the United States and Canada will experience the greatest ever intergenerational transfer of wealth from the elderly to their children and heirs. Many charities have scrambled to position themselves to benefit from this fact by launching planned giving programs.

Many view this newfound enthusiasm for planned giving as crass opportunism—and in some cases, it may well be! However, churches have always encouraged the faithful to consider stewardship and philanthropic giving as part of their estate planning. A "legacy of faith" is a gift which allows people to dispose of their estates in a manner consistent with the values and interests they embraced in life, and which will enable the Body of Christ in all its manifestations to meet the challenges of the future in continuing to do God's work on earth. There is compelling scriptural precedent for this:

> With great power the apostles gave their testimony to the resurrection of the Lord Jesus, and great grace was upon them all. There was not a needy person among them, for as many as owned lands or houses sold them and brought the proceeds of what was sold. They laid it at the apostles' feet, and it was distributed to each as any had need (Acts 4:33–35).

Until recently, most people thought of planned giving chiefly in terms of wills and bequests—testamentary gifts from the accumulated assets of their estate, normally executed at the time of death. However, these days, because of favorable tax treatment, and the unimaginable wealth baby boomers have accumulated during their lives, more and more people are engaging in *inter-vivos* charitable giving, or gifts made during the course of their lifetime. In this sense, planned giving has taken on a broader meaning. Although it does not preclude the possibility of a *cash* gift, it is most appropriately defined as "any gift requiring the assistance of a professional to transfer or administer." Therefore, planned gifts include, but are not limited to, the gift of publicly traded securities (stocks), which require the assistance of a trader; insurance products (annuities), which require an insurance agent; property (homes, farms, investment lands), which require a real estate agent; or a gift at death (a will), which requires a lawyer and/or executor.

Estate planning is something most people approach with great apprehension. Generally speaking, it requires us to discuss some of the most intimate details of our lives with professionals such as lawyers and financial planners. Discussing our own death and how we may wish to have our estate administered afterwards, requires us to contemplate our mortality, and the state of our relationships with others. How we dispose of our estates says much about us, our lives, and our values. Our estates, properly planned and distributed, can generously provide for the next generation of our families, friends, Christian ministries, the church, and people in need whom we may never have met—but who might have enjoyed our generosity had we been alive.

For Christians, there is an especially attractive universality about planned giving, in that almost everyone is capable of participating. Everyone, rich or poor, will create an estate during his or her lifetime. When we have embraced stewardship as a lifelong Christian value, planned giving provides a welcome opportunity to ensure that the church and those charities which have been important throughout our lives also figure in our estate planning considerations.

In this sense a *legacy of faith* allows us to project our values beyond the present and into the future. At its core is the conviction that we simply do not need all the resources we have amassed in life, no matter how much or how little, and that, whether in life or in death, we would like to return to God a portion of the bounty with which we have been entrusted. Generosity is not quantifiable, based on a measure of wealth, but is rather the willingness to respond to grace, and to use the abundance that comes from God for the good of the Body of Christ and humanity. Creating a legacy of faith is one way to fulfill the values inherent in the idea of Jubilee, by restoring opportunity, hope and resources to our brothers and sisters at the turn of every generation.

In addition to being consistent with the practice of our faith, a planned gift can in many instances be an important part of wise financial planning. As a matter of public policy, both Americans and Canadians have enjoyed significant expansions in the favorable tax treatment of planned gifts. In 2001, for example, through the leadership of organizations like the Canadian Association of Gift Planners (CAGP), Canada made permanent a 50% capital gains tax reduction on the gift of publicly traded securities to charities, including churches. In both the United States and Canada, a gift of such securities and other structured estate gifts can significantly reduce taxes at death, thereby ensuring that one's family and other heirs, such as the church and other Christian ministries, are the principal beneficiaries of one's life work. While favorable tax treatment will never be the motivation for making a charitable gift, the promotion of philanthropy in public policy can greatly encourage people to include planned generosity as part of their life-long commitment as passionate stewards. Remember, tax credits are not a reason to give. They may leverage giving. A joyful heart and the desire to be a passionate steward are always at the core of a generous gift, freely given.

The benefits of creating a legacy of faith during one's own lifetime are undeniable: most notable is the satisfaction of actually seeing a ministry you value receive support. However, it is important to recognize that not everyone who would like to make a planned gift is currently in a position to do so. Pensioners, for instance—who, as noted earlier, comprise an increasing percentage of the population—may be property-rich, but cash-poor. For these people, *testamentary* legacies of faith may be the ideal option.

Members of a church may thus choose either to create a legacy of faith that is fulfilled in their lifetime, or upon death. Regardless, what characterizes a legacy of faith is the intentional and deliberate provision of one's resources for the needs of the church and Christian ministries. There is a constancy here that is frequently missing in our response to crisis campaigns or even the annual "highlight on stewardship" appeal. Planned gifts add a dimension of longevity to our stewardship, by bringing our commitment to the future, and not just the present, or the remediation of the past, under the umbrella of our generosity.

In this respect, we need to note that the decision to create a legacy of faith is a choice based in trust. This is especially true of testamentary gifts, since none of us knows when we will die. This means we cannot predict when our gift will actually come into the hand of the church or other Christian ministry, nor exactly who will manage its disbursement, nor even what needs will loom largest in their eyes. Donors must trust that the Christian charities will be good stewards of their gift once received. And Christian charities, including churches, for their part have an obligation to be trustworthy. It should not surprise us that many of the faithful will scrutinize the church and other charities' current practice in order to assess how they might steward any gift in the future. For this reason, we are wise to take more seriously than ever our corporate responsibility to be good stewards of the gifts passionate stewards entrust to us.

Planning for the Future through Planned Giving

The Christian community's readiness to encourage planned giving, and the deliberate provision for the future that legacies of faith entail will be crucial for our long-term ability to meet the